C000260503

ONE NATION
power hope community

ONE NATION
power hope community

Edited by

Owen Smith & Rachel Reeves

London 2013

First published 2013

Published by One Nation Register
onenationregister@gmail.com

British Library Cataloguing in Publication Data
A catalogue record for this book is available from the British
Library

ISBN 9781 909831 001

Cover design: Fran Davies

Text setting E-type, Liverpool
Printed and bound by Halstan, Amersham

Contents

Preface

One Nation is a British idea rooted deep in our history and language. It is not a Conservative idea or a Labour idea.

People in this country have always believed strongly in everyone mucking in, pulling their weight, doing their bit and playing their part.

One Nation Labour lays down that challenge in our time. It is based on the idea that we can only rebuild Britain if everyone is given an opportunity to play their part, and if we demand that everyone shows their responsibilities to each other, right to the top of society.

At the heart of the idea of One Nation is a belief in us prospering together as a country. We will not tolerate a widening gap between the richest and poorest. The route to economic recovery will be through addressing the living standards crisis being suffered by millions of families, not through helping millionaires get richer still.

And a One Nation Labour Party is a party of the national interest, not one part of the country or any sectional interest. One Nation Labour reaches out so that individual voices from all over our country are heard in our party, from every walk of life, young and old, public and private sector, north and south.

For Britain to become One Nation we must do more than design a programme for government, because national renewal cannot be delivered by government alone. To build One Nation requires all of us – government, business, trade unions, councils, civil society, communities and individuals – to work together. All of us have a part to play, and only by uniting the country can we make that happen.

There was a time, not so long ago, when Conservatives echoed a similar sentiment about us being 'in it together'. But David Cameron's government is dividing our country: squeezing living standards for the many and rewarding a wealthy few at the top. In these circumstances, even these Conservatives are not quite bare-faced enough to maintain the pretence that they are a One Nation party.

But just as One Nation will mean a change from this Tory-led government, it will also mean a change from the last Labour government. The 2010 generation of Labour MPs who write in this volume are particularly well-placed to understand that. They recognise that we need to learn from our experience, our successes and our failures in office, and to apply fresh thinking to the times our country faces.

That is why this book is so important. These MPs, like so many of their colleagues from the 2010 intake and before, bring to our party a special connection with the people they represent.

These essays tell the story of their communities, their values, the personal routes that brought them into politics. They show how we need to renew Labour's traditions as a grassroots party of work, family and place if we are to earn the trust of the people again.

I am immensely proud to lead this new generation of Labour MPs.

I would like to thank the contributors for the time and care they put into their writing, and especially Rachel Reeves and Owen Smith for their initiative in putting together and editing this book.

Ed Miliband, August 2013

One Nation:
a country where everyone plays their part, a country we rebuild together

Owen Smith and Rachel Reeves

Most of those gathered to hear Ed Miliband's speech at the Labour Party conference in 2012 recognised that under his leadership the party had become an effective and united Opposition. They also knew that fresh scandals over top pay, consumer rip-offs and banking sharp practices had vindicated his call for a more responsible capitalism, and that his analysis of the problems facing the squeezed middle and the need for deep reforms in the economy had struck a chord with millions of voters.

But it is only fair to say that some of those present in Manchester had voiced doubts about how Ed could draw all this together into an overarching political project.

Those doubts were swiftly dispelled by an extra-ordinary speech, delivered without notes. Ed Miliband rose to the challenge, as he had done in the past. The theme of his speech, a closely guarded secret until he stood up, was a vision for rebuilding Britain as One

Nation: 'A country where everyone has a stake; a country where prosperity is fairly shared; where we have a shared destiny, a sense of shared endeavour and a common life that we lead together.'

This was not just an audacious land-grab of a phrase once associated with a more compassionate era of Conservative government. Nor was he describing some impossible dream. Instead, the speech addressed, full on, the challenges facing Britain today.

'Here is the genius of One Nation', he told the Conference:

> It doesn't just tell us the country we can be. It tells us how we must rebuild. We won the war because we were One Nation. We built the peace because Labour governments and Conservative understood we needed to be One Nation. Every time Britain has faced its gravest challenge, we have only come through the storm because we were One Nation ... To overcome the challenges we face, we must rediscover that spirit. That spirit the British people never forgot. That spirit of One Nation.

Since that speech, Ed Miliband and the shadow cabinet have been setting out what this means for our economy, our society, and our politics: a recovery made by and for the many, not the few; a society in which everyone has the opportunity, and the responsibility, to take part; and a party and a democracy that is open to everyone, not the preserve of closed circles or a narrow elite.

The building blocks of One Nation include not only new policies but also a radical process of party reform. Labour is renewing itself as a movement and helping to give a voice to people from every part of Britain and every walk of life. These changes will underpin the next Labour government, so that we can work with citizens, communities, businesses and civil society to meet together the challenges we face together.

Labour has already set out a series of radical new proposals that show how a One Nation government could begin rebuilding Britain, together with the people of our country: policies to get our banks working for our businesses, and our businesses fulfilling their responsibilities to their customers and employees; policies to ensure our public services give young people a fair chance to play their part and our elderly population the dignity and care they deserve; policies for the redesign of our tax and social security system so that everyone pays their fair share and responsibility goes all the way from the bottom to the top; policies to reform and renew our politics so that we can begin to reverse the disaffection and hopelessness that discourages too many from taking part. And of course the Labour Party will have more to say about all this and more before the next election.

But this is not a book about policy, or a blueprint for political reform. Instead, these essays show how our policy programme and our campaign for the chance to implement it in government are anchored in people's everyday lives, experiences, aspirations and struggles.

Ed Miliband has argued that if we are to be a one-term Opposition, and to succeed as a One Nation government, we must not only learn from the experience of the last Labour government – we must also look beyond it.

That is why it is significant this book is a collection of essays written by recently elected MPs. All our contributors were elected at the last general election or in by-elections since. The freshness and energy of their ideas show how Ed's leadership has galvanised the Labour Party and the new generation of MPs.

They also offer further evidence of the deep resonance of the values of One Nation – and not just within the Labour Party. Our values are vividly present in so many of the personal stories and local histories that make up our country. The brilliant, resilient and resourceful people and communities of Britain are ready and eager to play their part in rebuilding our country as One Nation.

But there is also a humility in the vision of One Nation, and the ideas running through this book: we understand that governments, on their own, cannot fix everything. This humility, though born in opposition, will continue when we are in government. We know that

Labour will not be able to deliver the change Britain needs unless we make it a common endeavour – unless we work with families and communities, businesses and trade unions, civic society and elected leaders at every level. The fundamental renewal of Labour's values, organisation, and approach to politics and social change, is the most important and transformative part of Ed Miliband's project – a renewal to which all these chapters testify.

**

In their contributions, Catherine McKinnell, Rushanara Ali, Rachel Reeves and Owen Smith all draw on local and personal experiences to demonstrate the immediate relevance to the lives of so many people today of Ed Miliband's proposals for building a more inclusive and balanced economy. They also show us that there are people everywhere ready to rise to the call of building that new economy and stronger society together.

Shabana Mahmood and Gloria De Piero report on the ways in which they are responding to Ed's challenge to re-engage with people and open up our party and our politics to new forces, through enabling new leaders and creating stronger communities.

Dan Jarvis reflects on the ways in which the idea of One Nation can draw on and develop the value of serving one's country – and how this can enrich our approach to economic development, community empowerment and public service reform.

Lilian Greenwood and Kate Green argue that we cannot succeed as a country when society is damaged and divided by widening inequality – and when too many children lack a fair chance to play their part in our future.

Steve Reed, formerly a council leader on the frontline of public service reform and community empowerment, describes ways in which services can be improved and social problems tackled when users and producers, politicians and communities, and the public, private and voluntary sectors, all have a chance to play their part.

Finally, Tristram Hunt, who worked as a historian before he entered Parliament, shows that this project is one with deep roots in the traditions of our party and other movements; but he also shows how Ed Miliband's new synthesis draws on these traditions to offer radical solutions to today's most pressing problems.

Through all these different perspectives, there is a strong thread of common values, a consistent critique, and a shared vision. All these new MPs understand that power has become too concentrated in the hands of elites, in the state or in the market, and needs to be dispersed and devolved; restoring real accountability and responsibility to the people of Britain.

They share a vision of a country in which our economy

delivers for everyone, not just those with the most; where government understands its duty to business, and business its duty to society; where public services are designed with their users; and where people can once more believe in their politics and their politicians.

Together these chapters show why Ed Miliband's call for everyone to play their part in rebuilding Britain as One Nation has struck such a chord. They show that the spirit of fairness, social responsibility and collective commitment that he has invoked not only echoes through our history but is today more relevant than ever as we face our challenges as a nation. They show that, as well as having deep roots in the history of the labour movement, these values have the potential to excite and unite the broad majority of the British people. They show the urgency, at a time of deepening division and disengagement, of the Labour Party rising to this challenge.

The task is formidable and the responsibility a heavy one. But these essays also give solid grounds for courage and confidence – for the good news is that, under Ed Miliband's leadership, and with the best of our movement and our country to draw on, the work has already begun.

1. Our common aim

Owen Smith

I grew up mostly in Pontypridd, a coal town once and a
market town still, in the Valley where the Taff and
Rhondda rivers meet. Politics runs through my
community like the railway that once ran coal to Barry
Docks, and from there to the cities of the industrial
revolution. It's a politics of strong passions and
convictions, loyalty and decency, solidarity and security,
family and community: a politics that understands the
value of place and people and power. It's Labour, of
course, and has been since 1922, when T.I. Mardy Jones
was elevated from the pit face to parliament.

Those values and that loyalty persist in Pontypridd, as
they do in similar communities right across the UK. But
they have been tested in recent years, as never before.
Declining industry has stunted wealth and opportunity,
and fragmented neighbours, families and generations.
Political disappointments, too, have frayed the edges of
my community. The social and economic changes we
have experienced have diminished trust and faith in
progress and politics, and these have been replaced for
too many by a nagging sense of loss, apathy and

sometimes anger. We hear it on the doorstep in that anti-rallying cry of our age: 'Why bother voting? You're all the same anyway'.

One Nation Labour is the answer to that scarring charge, an antidote to the apathy. One Nation Labour is animating a new and hungry generation of Labour men and women, and restoring faith in our politics. It thrives on a belief in progress for our people, and optimism about the future – for all of our people, not just those with the most. One Nation Labour is more than a slogan, or even a strategy. It acknowledges what is wrong with the state of our nation – the faults that are crystal clear to most of us but have for so long seemed obscure to the dominant political classes. And it seeks to tackle them: the concentration of power among self-perpetuating elites, away from the people, which has gradually undermined trust in previously well-loved institutions; the growing inequality that has hardened dividing lines between the wealthiest and the rest; and the economic growth whose benefits have not been distributed fairly across our country and its people.

One Nation Labour understands the scale of the crisis we face – a crisis that is also evident in many more prosperous parts of the country than Pontypridd – and is putting in place the policies to deal with it. Too many are out of work, while those in it have little time for anything else. Prices are too high and wages too low. Public services are more vital than ever, yet trust in their efficiency is at an all-time low. And at a time when politics should be all the more important, faith in its ability to deliver change is strikingly absent.

The solutions to these challenges are the same whether in Pontypridd or in posher places. We need markets that work in consumers' interests as well as those of share-holders; companies that pay their taxes; and wages that can sustain a family. We need a state that pursues full employment alongside a falling deficit, and rules that govern fair markets as well as freedom of enterprise; and we need public services that inspire trust at home and envy abroad. We cannot afford to succumb to false choices – between aspiration and equality, credibility and radicalism, leadership and grass-roots reform. One Nation Labour must deliver all of these. This has been Ed Miliband's call to our party and to Britain: for a politics of national renewal that is rooted in the reality of every community of the country and reaches out to people across every walk of life.

The roots of our politics

This should not be mistaken for a year-zero approach. One Nation was not born from a single conference speech. Its roots lie deep in our heritage, and in that of the wider movement of which we are a part. Labour has always been about community and collective ambition, work for all and wages worth working for. Labour has always been about progress for the many, and the means to achieve it. Labour has always been about power, and winning it to give it back to the people. One Nation Labour draws on these traditions but shapes them in a way that works in the twenty-first century.

Pontypridd isn't a bad place to start in this project of revisiting our history. From the town's raucous Victorian beginnings, through to its Edwardian pomp and then the first inklings of decline in the mid-1920s, its migrant population has always worked to build a community of real power and conviction – one that can still inspire. Walk down its main streets, and the ambition and optimism of that earlier age is everywhere to see: municipal buildings of elegance and substance, parklands and bandstands, schools and chapels, libraries and a lido. They speak of the relative wealth of the society that built them, of course, but more importantly of its passion for progress, its culture of participation and its collective aspiration and energy. And though bricks and mortar may be the physical legacy of those ambitions, their real achievements were the human and political structures that we built to deliver them, and the common good they symbolised. There were friendly societies and the co-op, miners' lodges and the Fed, unions and the Labour Party.

Politics, then, was a new religion: our most potent credo was the faith that when we organise ourselves we can shape our world.

That spirit of common engagement was still powerful in the Pontypridd I knew in the 1970s and early 1980s, even as light industry and the Royal Mint (moved to Wales by Labour) replaced the pits, and the chain-works that had fitted out the Titanic. But things are not quite like that any more. The social and economic shifts of the last thirty years have slowly eroded many of the structures that held us together – the workplace, the chapel, the unions and the party. And for too many there has also been an erosion of the very idea of a common good and a political fight to achieve it. In Ponty, as elsewhere, collectivism has been trumped by consumerism, common responsibilities by individual rights. And our politics – in particular the fortunes of the local Labour Party, once the fulcrum and catalyst for community action – is reflective of the trend. Membership and majorities are counted carefully now, when once they were weighed. Belief in our mission is dwindling.

How do we turn this around and renew political engagement, a faith in progress, and a belief in Labour as its vehicle? That was the key question for me when I was elected in 2010, and it remains the central issue today. I believe the answer comes in two parts: we need both bottom-up participation and leadership from the top; to simultaneously cultivate our roots and command the heights. And One Nation Labour is determined to achieve both these things.

Commanding the heights

Leadership starts with a clear-eyed analysis of the ways in which not only our economy and society have changed, but also our politics. For the scale of our politics, its scope and ambition, has itself been a contributor to the current crisis. As we confronted the new challenges of multinational money and global markets, our politics was shrunk to fit the limited ambitions for government action that have become orthodox political and economic wisdom – neoliberalism, if you like. This great contraction of ambition began in the 1970s, as the golden era of post-war growth finally came to an end. The idea that people in one country could shape the future through their government began to appear – certainly to those on the right – to be a dangerous illusion. The effects of this new orthodoxy were felt everywhere, in theory and in practice. Full employment became an impossible dream – unachievable we were told, without triggering Weimar-like inflation. Unemployment, by contrast, was a price worth paying. Regulation of the banks or the markets, of workers' rights or minimum room sizes – the safety valves and safety nets hard won in the half-century before – was abandoned in pursuit of flexibility. Inequality, once a moral affront, became a necessary evil, a by-product of the new entrepreneurialism that would surely, eventually, lift all boats.

But it was the trickery of trickle-down economics, not the power of government, that proved to be the real illusion. And though their sleight of hand was finally and devastatingly exposed in the global crash of 2008-9, it had, in truth, been a long con, whose real sting had already been seen in the widening gulf in opportunities and outcomes for individuals and regions across Britain. The abandonment of political ambition had allowed a bonanza for the elite at the expense of the many.

In the past many leading Tories have also recognised the damage that can result from a divided society. It was Disraeli who first pointed to the problem of 'two nations', and Macmillan's paternalism shared with post-war Labour governments the optimism that politicians could make a difference – that together, sometimes as small platoons and at other times as the big state, we could secure collective improvement for the many not the few. That ended with Thatcherism. Disraeli's desire to heal the two nations – whose division, he said, denied the 'community of purpose that constitutes society' – gave way to Thatcher's assertion that there was no such thing.

New Labour was no continuation of Thatcher, as our opponents like to tease. Our Labour governments from 1997 to 2010 sought to address inequality through programmes of investment in sinking public services, a focus on child poverty, delivery of the minimum wage and other protections for workers, and our human rights legislation. All these were anathema to Tory ideology, as their current unwinding shows. But, as Ed Miliband has made clear as party leader, these measures were not enough to build One Nation. The next Labour government will have to do more than find accommodation with the market: we must bend it to the people's will.

Good markets are a vital means of distributing resources efficiently, but they must work for all of the people – not just those in the know. And good government acknowledges that it has real responsibilities to the markets – and that these involve much more than simply getting out of their way. Good governments tackle the market's worst excesses, but their responsibilities go beyond that to include building an economy that serves the people and contributes to our wellbeing. So One Nation Labour wants workers to have a wage that you can raise a family on, not just a basic minimum. It asks those who benefit from access to markets, decent infrastructure and a trained workforce to give something back in return. It puts consumers first, even when that requires reform of sectors with powerful vested interests. And it believes that good government can make a difference.

Responsible capitalism requires a society where government understands its duty to business, and business remembers it has a duty to society. One Nation Labour's leadership on this agenda is already clear. We will reform failing markets, as in energy. We will incentivise an investment culture that builds long-term value not quick-fire profit. We will bring down the deficit with an approach that is rooted in a fair sharing of burdens. We will spread the opportunity for growth and decentralise decision-making through regional banks and powerful local government. And we will prioritise high employment and a balanced economy. In committing to do these things, One Nation Labour is restating – or perhaps rediscovering – its faith in the power of government, and it is inviting the British people, through their party, to take back power for themselves.

Community power

But leadership from above, however necessary, radical and credible, will not suffice. Disillusion and division is too deep at the grassroots of our nation to be overcome with top-down reform on its own. If One Nation Labour is to convince, and then to succeed, we must also rediscover our ability to organise and catalyse from below. That is why we have set about refounding Labour as a party rooted in real lives and communities, and one which hears the voices of working people. Here, too, our heritage holds the key: we need to bring its lessons to bear in new ways of working and connecting with our communities.

You might think it would be an easier task to revive participative traditions in Pontypridd, with its proud identity and deep history of community and co-operation, than in some other parts of Britain, where a sense of place and politics is perhaps harder to locate. However, in the three years since I was elected the means to galvanise that engagement has proved elusive and frustrating. This is undoubtedly partly a result of the many previous false dawns that have promised progress but failed to deliver: it's hard to feel progressive when there seems so little sign of progress for you and yours. But it also partly stems from that self-same culture of can-do self-reliance – which can sometimes itself confound greater co-operation and common purpose. Very local campaigns – the Friends of the Park, the protection of the paddling pool, the resurrection of the rugby club – can seem more realistic and rewarding than the great causes they have tended to supplant. However I believe that small successes also have the capacity to generate the confidence to progress to bigger projects, if people have the time, support and skills to shape their community.

This means that giving our young people the tools to become citizens of the future is part of the equation for a new politics. But we also need somehow to shift our own culture so that it becomes one that motivates and inspires people to go beyond the daily routine of the desk, the supermarket and the front room. Protecting family time through proper wages and changing workplace culture is a prerequisite, but it is also vital that we reconnect local energy and local communities to the politics that is meant to serve them, that we restore lines of communication, and a belief that politics can deliver.

On these issues too there are lessons we can learn from past Labour actions in government and current practice in opposition. In government, Labour delivered devolution to Wales, after one hundred years of campaigning, and in so doing it helped forge a new dynamic of common national purpose, and a new proximity between the people and those in power. And although the process of devolution is still unfolding, and the divisions of responsibility between local, Welsh and British strata are still works in progress, there is now a renewed sense of ownership of government institutions in Wales, and a greater perception of transparency and accountability. One Nation Labour is learning from these lessons, and seeking again to win power in order to give it away – to devolved, democratic control in local and national government, across all parts of the UK.

We also understand that it is not just in Westminster and in government that we can build a One Nation future. Already, in opposition, Labour is remaking itself as a community party. Always a synthesiser of ideas and interests, Labour is borrowing from Barack Obama as we've borrowed from Benjamin Disraeli. The community organising principles that were developed by the forerunners of Labour in the Rochdale Pioneers and the Miners Lodges of the Valleys, and long ago crossed the Atlantic, are now coming back again, via Chicago and Arnie Graf, Citizens UK and Movement for Change. Iain McNicol has been leading reforms in the party aimed at building a more open and inclusive movement. Slowly but surely, Labour is re-engaging with dialogue in our communities, and developing new common objectives and solutions that will prove the real foundations for our rebuilding.

Our councillors must be in the vanguard of these activities: they have the necessary tools for pushing services closer to the communities they serve and giving people a real say in their delivery. Whether through devolving community budgets to individual estates or communities of interest, redesigning services hand in hand with working people, or having the foresight in difficult times to protect important cultural, arts and leisure facilities, Labour activists in local government hold the keys that can once more unlock civic pride.

Steve Reed, a former council leader, describes in his chapter how co-operative councils, led by Labour, are doing just that. Their activities are a guiding light for Labour councils right across the UK. Our politics, at a local and national level, must be more responsive to, and welcoming of, the energy and innovation in communities that often sits outside party political activities, but could and should be used to improve them.

That process of community renewal and grass-roots energy is evident in Pontypridd. It can be seen, for example, in community campaigns to create fan-owned rugby clubs – so as to wrest our sporting birthrights back from money men and the markets – and in broader efforts to create alternative forums for discussion and agreement on local priorities.

Pontypridd Citizens, which will bring together churches and parties, unions and residents, in order to determine local needs and empower local leaders, is launching this year, taking its cue and its form from similar schemes that are energising communities across Britain. It will mark a new beginning in the politics of Pontypridd, and Labour will be at its heart.

One nation once more

In big ways and small, One Nation Labour will remake our ability to come together, as communities and as a country. Recognising the scale of the inequality that squeezes the living standards of all but the very richest, One Nation Labour is working to tackle the issue through rebuilding our economy and society with a politics of the common good. It seeks a politics of inclusion not division, of activism not apathy – and of credibility and radicalism. That is the bold challenge that Ed Miliband's leadership has set us: to rebuild together as One Nation. This is a challenge that is equal to the scale of the economic and social ills of our age. And it is both an end and a means, because it will require everyone to play their part. It is also one that would have seemed familiar to many others:

> We have lived so long at the mercy of uncontrolled economic forces that we have become sceptical regarding any plan for human emancipation ... for all of the people ... The question is not really whether we are intelligent enough to plan our social life, but whether we are good enough to restrain the selfish passions that divide us, and wise enough to co-operate for the realisation of a common aim ... and safeguard democracy by lifting the conditions

of our people to a higher level of material wellbeing and cultural opportunity.

Macmillan not Miliband. 1937 not 2013. But nonetheless an expression of our values: British values, progressive values, One Nation values – and values that today are cherished only by the Labour Party.

Owen Smith is MP for Pontypridd, and Labour's shadow secretary of state for Wales. Before being elected he was a BBC journalist, a special adviser in Northern Ireland and a company director in the Biotechnology Industry.

2. Knock knock, Who cares?

Gloria De Piero

One of the reasons I love being an MP is that I'm constantly reminded that politics still has the power to surprise. Even a regular door-knocking session, when it's done slightly differently, can yield unpredictable results. Last month I decided to conduct a simple experiment in my constituency in Ashfield. The lessons we learned are valuable ones for our party. Like most others across the country, our team regularly knocks on doors and asks people how they would vote if there was a general election tomorrow. The idea, of course, is to identify Labour voters, so we can get them out to vote on polling day.

My register tells me that in Ashfield, as in many parts of the country, about 40 per cent of residents don't bother to vote. Usually we would ignore those people, and focus only on the likely Labour voters. But on this occasion I turned the normal process on its head. I passed by the doors of those who vote and instead engaged with the non-voters. I tried to say as little as possible – I wanted the conversation to be led by them. I wanted to listen rather than talk. I also wanted to record as much of what they said as possible. I expected to hear that all us politicians are the same, and to have doors slammed in my face. But my expectations were wrong. I ended up talking about – well – politics.

That evening I met 34-year-old Shaun, who told me: 'I did vote Labour twice but I haven't voted for five or six years'. His partner, 40-year-old Donna, said: 'I don't vote. If I did, it would be Labour, but I can't be arsed'. Donna and Shaun both worked full-time, although Donna was one of hundreds of local warehouse workers serving out their redundancy notices. Shaun commented: 'Everything is just going up, but wages don't go up'. Donna told me about the lack of shops in the Kirkby-in-Ashfield precinct, and the traffic congestion that now stops many potential customers from going there. I asked Donna, who clearly cared passionately about her town, if she'd ever consider being a councillor. She said she wouldn't. 'It's the way we've been brought up. We're like a *Shameless* family. We're a big family. If we turned up on the doorstep no one would vote for us.' Then she paused for a moment and reflected on what she had just said. 'Actually, maybe there should be some people like us on the council. It affects us'. I'd spent about five or six minutes with Donna and Shaun but I felt that we'd travelled a long way in that time.

Next I met 22-year-old chef Dave. 'I used to vote

Labour but not since expenses', he said. 'Some people spent more on a lunch than I earn in a day'. He was understandably angry with politicians, and I tentatively suggested he should have a go at doing the job himself. 'I'd like to do it but it would never happen', he replied. 'I'm dyslexic. I've got nothing to offer. I've got no connections. I don't know anyone.' Dave's words affected me profoundly – as they would any Labour MP. I might as well have suggested he become a High Court judge. That can't be right. Earlier in our chat Dave had told me: 'How can you understand what their policies are when people use big long words? It goes over my head'. He is right to raise this issue. Is it really so difficult for politicians to communicate ideas in a clear and concise way, without reaching for jargon and buzzwords that aren't used by anyone but us.

Next I met Chris, 29 and his wife Michelle, 34. They told me bluntly they weren't interested in politics, and then starting talking to me about ... politics. Michelle told me that her husband worked sixty hours a week. She felt aggrieved that working families aren't treated properly, while 'them that don't do anything have cars'. She continued: 'I don't really understand politics. I know the rich get richer and the poor poorer. I understand that. I'd vote Labour but I don't vote. I hate him that's in though.' Michelle also talked about the need for parents to be responsible, and not to allow their children out at night unsupervised, and about the ways in which anti-social behaviour affects the neighbourhood.

I asked whether, since she was so passionate about the issues, she'd ever consider getting involved in local politics. Perhaps one day she'd like to serve on the council? I didn't record at the time whether it was Michelle or Chris who replied. Perhaps the words cut through me, and I was distracted by the power of what they said. 'We feel thick. We're little people', they replied. But after a moment's silence Michelle said: 'Actually I think I could do it'. It made me sad and frustrated that I didn't feel able to invite them to a Labour Party meeting. I knew they would feel just as alienated there. Not by the wonderful members of Ashfield Labour Party. But they'd be alienated by all the bureaucracy and formality: the discussion of the minutes, the apologies and the show of hands. In truth I don't think anyone enjoys traditional Labour Party meetings. We've actually had meetings to discuss what we do about meetings. Seriously.

Locked out voters

I realise this is simply a snapshot of a few streets in Ashfield, but work that I carried out earlier this year also showed that there's an appetite out there to get involved in politics – and even to enter Parliament – but that people don't have the faintest idea where to start. The truth is that for too long we have locked people out.

Given that trust in politics and politicians is at an all-time low, what percentage of people would you expect to be interested in standing for Parliament? – one in a hundred? one in ten? In fact, polling carried out for me earlier this year by YouGov (with a sample size of 1633) showed that the answer is nearly one in four. That is much higher than I would ever have imagined.

The question posed by YouGov was:

> Imagine you were in your thirties or forties, and friends of yours suggested you should stand for election to become an MP. What do you think your reaction would be?

Six per cent of those polled chose the response 'Enthusiastic: I'd definitely consider standing', while 18 per cent ticked the box for 'Interested: I might consider standing'. This gives a total percentage of those either enthusiastic or interested of 24 per cent.

So nearly one in four people would be interested in standing for Parliament. But the problem is – as I heard in my 'Why Do People Hate Me?' tour earlier this year, when I asked groups of people how they'd feel about becoming a politician – hardly anyone knows how to go about it.

During that tour, 24-year-old Liam Jones, a warehouse delivery driver in Derbyshire, commented: 'It's not in the Job Centre or anything like that, is it? It's not, though, so how do you know where to start?' His colleague Sharon, who is in her fifties, packed boxes at the same warehouse. 'It's not advertised, is it? You don't pick a paper up and it says "one politician wanted, come for this interview", do you?'

I explained to Frank from Nottinghamshire, who is in his thirties and recently lost his job at an aerospace engineering firm, that becoming a councillor was a question of representing your community, and that no academic qualifications were needed. His eyes lit up, and he asked me how he could do it. I told him to contact his local constituency chairperson and to go along to a meeting that usually takes place on a Friday night. I knew I had lost Frank. I had him for a moment. But as soon as I told him what the next step was, he looked at me as if I was mad.

Luke, Sharon and Frank all raise perfectly sensible points. How would you know how to become a candidate for a political party unless a family member or mentor was involved, or unless someone had actively recruited you? For the vast majority of people, neither of these possibilities is very likely.

Ed Miliband has declared his determination to open up the Labour Party and let the people back into politics.

He knows it cannot be a game conducted by a few for a few. As he said in his 2012 conference speech, One Nation is country where everyone plays their part. And that in turn means that people from all walks of life must feel able to play their part; and it means restating what politics is about.

When I asked each of the groups I visited on my tour what qualities were needed to become a politician, they all said 'qualifications', or 'a university education'. There was genuine surprise and scepticism when I told them that no academic qualifications were needed – that all that is required is a desire to represent your community. But we can only open up our movement by reaching out to those people and communities. Could we imagine an advert in the local paper along the following lines?

Do you have experience of representing people through a parents and teachers association, neighbourhood watch scheme or similar group, or by being a workplace rep? Maybe you have a good business head and would like to use your skills and knowledge to give something back to your community? If you share the Labour Party's values of fairness and opportunity for all you could have a go at being selected as a Labour Party candidate for the Council elections in XXXXXX. Candidates will be interviewed by fellow local Labour members, and must be a Labour Party member for 12 months before they are eligible to stand. Half of all the chosen candidates will be women. Allowances are Xk a year.

One Nation participation

Ed Miliband is now applying One Nation principles to the urgent task of Labour Party reform. As he said in his July 2013 speech, we need to do more, not less, to make individual trade union members part of our party: the three million shopworkers, nurses, engineers, bus drivers and construction workers who are members of Labour affiliated trade unions – people from the public and private sector alike. Their individual voices need to be heard louder and clearer than ever before.

Anyone who thinks that these ordinary working men and women dominate the Labour Party – its selections, elections and decision-making – are not living in the real world. They are barely involved at all, and are certainly not properly part of all that we do.

The vast majority are not members of local parties. But having a proper relationship with these members would give us access to the biggest and best focus group, one that other political parties could only dream of. We could start by contacting them and asking them what their priorities are. But if we want them to be actively involved there needs to be more than a boring meeting, a letter asking them for cash or an invitation to take part in a door-knocking session. We need to give them genuine opportunities to get involved in the ways their neighbourhoods are run and their communities are represented.

The changes Ed is driving through in our relationship with individual trade union members go hand in hand with the bottom-up organisational reforms already being overseen by Arnie Graf and Iain McNicol. We are becoming a grass-roots party once more, delivering real change on the doorstep with community organisers – not just leaflets through letter boxes.

It is partly because of my own experiences that since entering Parliament I have focused on disengagement from politics. There is a simple reason I became a journalist. After serving for a year as an elected National Labour Students Officer I couldn't get a job in politics. I contacted think tanks, put myself forward for party roles and applied for research assistant roles. But I got nowhere. We in the Labour Party have to ask ourselves how it could be that it was easier for me to forge a successful career in the media than it was to work in progressive politics. I don't want to sound chippy, but I felt that no-one around Westminster looked or sounded like me. My story is just one of many, but it is currently far too difficult for people from ordinary backgrounds to enter politics.

To end on a positive note – the YouGov poll on standing for election had some good news for the Labour Party: it was people who had voted Labour at the 2010 election who were the most likely to be enthusiastic or interested in standing as an MP, and were least likely to say 'I don't like politicians and the way politics works'. There's all to play for if we can create a One Nation politics that looks and sounds like Britain.

There's also a particular responsibility on Labour to say that enough is enough. That we will do more than continue to fight the other parties for our share of an ever dwindling number of votes. We are One Nation Labour. We aspire to represent the whole community because we know that Britain can only prosper when we are a country where everyone plays their part and has their voice heard. We will not practise the divisive sectionalism of the Tories, and so we will knock on every door. It may take a lot of listening to others before people are willing to listen to us. But we must tackle the disillusionment head-on. And in this Ed has set us on the right course. After all, if we don't open up politics for the many, who will?

Gloria De Piero is MP for Ashfield, and a shadow home office minister. Before entering parliament she worked in television and radio, including for the BBC's *On the Record* and *Politics Show*, and as GMTV's political editor.

3. Community, power and hope

Shabana Mahmood

Representing the area you grew up in is a privilege, but there are also high stakes. This is the area that has helped to make you who you are, so you want to do good job. It is not enough simply to represent – as an MP with deep roots in the community you want to agitate for change. That is what you are there for. At least, that is how I understood the job description.

I was born in the Small Heath area of my constituency. I grew up here. I went to school here. I live here still (well, until the last boundary review – I am now a full 106 yards outside the boundary, but you get the point).

I know my constituency. I am an inner city Brummie. It is the core of who I am. I know the vibrancy of the small businesses that pepper the main roads, and the stories of the people who run them. The classrooms of the local comprehensive, bursting at the seams as a result of its growing reputation for excellence, are all familiar to me; so too is the sense of community and responsibility that means that people look out for each other and check in on elderly neighbours, and the many small acts of kindness that make a big impact.

But I also know the problems that come round again and again. As soon as one problem is solved, another arrives. Or – even worse – the same problem comes back in a different form. These are the nagging thorns in the side of local residents, who year on year lose faith in the political system that is supposed to serve them. In their reality the system is something that does things to them. Often these are things they neither wanted nor asked for, and occasionally they are things that frankly defy common sense, that could only have been dreamt up by someone with no clue about what life here is really like.

And every time the system lets residents down, hope, belief and optimism all take a collective battering, and communities begin to accept that things are the way they are … well, because they are.

And politicians inevitably take a battering too. How much hope has to have been lost before a resident will tell you with a straight face that you're only there on their doorstep because there's an election … even when it's the end of May and the next election is almost twelve months away.

This is a constant refrain. It is time to do something about it. And this is what One Nation politics is all about.

So what can an MP do? What can I do?

When I am knocking on doors in the streets where I played as a child, hearing this frustration is gut-wrenching, because when communities lose hope – when they believe that the system is rigged against them – they also lose the power to effect change. As Samuel Smiles long ago observed, hope is the companion of power and the mother of success. Hope is what sustains us when we are down; it is what enables us to fight on when all looks lost.

This is why it was so important to me that hope was at the heart of Ed Miliband's conference speech in 2012. As he argued then, people need to believe in a vision for the future that we can build together. Hope is at the heart of One Nation politics.

So how do I, as a local MP, help the community resist this decline in hope, and how do I do my bit to support community power?

Theoretically, I am elected as a legislator, and as an advocate for individuals in their relationship with the institutions of the state. But, three years into the job, I am pretty sure that that is not enough. And it is not enough because the system is not working – at least not for the people I represent. Despite all the much lauded attempts to give power back to the people – whether through 'localism', 'devolution' or 'choice' – the power to get the things done that they want done still eludes people in my constituency.

Honestly, if the community in my patch really had power, would the derelict land at the top of Eversley Road – a place that is a magnet for drugs and anti-social behaviour – still lie idle? No. They would have taken it back from the land-owner who bought it hoping to make a quick buck. They would have put it into the kind of use I remember, when kids used to play there, or they would have built more affordable homes on it, for a community which is stretched to bursting point.

But community power, it seems, is in short supply. So although supporting hope and power may not in the past have been seen as central to a politician's job description, today it is increasingly part of our role. And here Ed Miliband's call for a national renewal in which we can all play our part is a crucial inspiration. Rebuilding Britain can and must begin locally: the collective endeavour that is part of our daily lives can then become part of the foundation of the way our country is run.

Leaders matter

When I was eleven, like many children in Birmingham I took the eleven-plus. Like many children I failed and went to the local comprehensive, Small Heath School. What did I learn? I learnt that setbacks happen, but that the end goal need not be in doubt. I still carried out my childhood dream of going to Oxford and becoming a barrister (as a teenager I wanted to be Kavanagh QC), before being elected to Parliament in 2010.

But I also learnt that individuals matter. Leaders matter.

While I was at Small Heath School the head teacher was beginning the slow and tortuous process of turning the school around. Mr Knight didn't sugar-coat the truth, but he also left us in no doubt that things would (eventually) come good. When I started as a pupil the school's results were below average, few parents were thrilled to be sending their kids there, and the school itself could barely cope with the many and varied challenges of serving one of the most deprived areas in the country.

But Mr Knight – and his successor Mr Slough – refused to give up. Their desire to strive for the best for 'our kids' was infectious. And now, sixteen years after I left, the school has just received its fourth successive 'Outstanding' rating from Ofsted. This is a stunning achievement, a testament to the leadership of individuals who chose to do the right thing ahead of the easy thing – leaders who understood the power of hope. The great men and women of history and of change are not, it transpires, the heroic giants of Thomas Carlyle. They are

people here in my constituency who are keeping hope
alive and empowering young people to live their dreams.

And there are more of them out there. And if they
could be found, and if they could be supported, I am
convinced that their impact on their community could be
as profound, as long lasting and as memorable as that of
Mr Knight and Mr Slough.

I have recently embarked on a neighbourhood-wide
engagement programme, in part aimed at doing just that.
Key to that has been a major effort to revitalise hope in a
population that has a pretty low opinion of politicians.
And we have found that through working relentlessly on
the smaller issues, being present when there's no election
in sight, and sticking to some modest but clear
commitments, we have been able to bring residents out in
droves to talk about how we could change our
community for the better; and this has included types of
people we don't always hear from – elderly and middle-
aged Muslim women, the teenagers who yearn for
community as much as anyone else.

Scratch away at the surface of despair and there sits
hope. Once engaged, people in my constituency were
quick to move away from thinking that sorting things out
was down to me, or them, or the council or the police –
almost straightaway the conversation was about we, the
collective, all of us together. And as the conversation
evolved, scores of people volunteered to come on this

journey, though they knew it would not be easy. There are no quick fixes for the problems that plague our area.

Residents have now stepped forward to become street champions, as part of a 'Street Champions Project'. In retrospect, a better choice of word might have been street leaders – because that is what they are, and that is what we need.

Knowledge is power

And what is my role in this? On one level it is straightforward. To help the volunteers set some priorities and some goals, to help them get the training they need, and to make sure that the agencies responsible for our area (the council, the police etc) work with them so that they succeed.

But the most important thing that I can do, I believe, is to empower these volunteers by sharing the knowledge that I have gained about how to get things fixed and make things happen. Remember, I'm from here – but I know what they don't know. I have made a start (and it is a grim process) on finding paths through the knowledge-maze that is all too often used as a weapon against ordinary people by the institutions which are supposed to serve them.

This is the knowledge that these street champions need to get things done – the name and number of the person you need to hassle in order to get something moved onto a list where it might actually be looked at, so that you don't get stuck in the ten layers of buffer around that person that are designed to filter out ordinary people. Or how to navigate the (often complex and convoluted) processes used by service providers to deliver their service – which you need to know before you can work out the quickest way to by-pass them to get stuff fixed.

Power in this sense comes from knowing the who, the what, and the how.

In my experience this is knowledge that is often second nature to politicians who live on the periphery of the real world (we know it's true – no one else really watches Marr at 9am on a Sunday). But it is not easy to access from the outside.

Politicians always talk about power. Mostly, it seems to me, we spend our time explaining that we don't have it! We occasionally misunderstand, and almost always fail to communicate, the nature of the power that we do have. It's not a 'click your fingers and hey presto' sort of power. It's a power to motivate, inform, connect, jostle, and co-operate, in the service of a better way. It is the power that comes from a refusal to give up or give in.

Some politicians talk of power as something they want to give away – especially when they want to avoid responsibility or unpopularity or both. And some talk about people power as choice, forgetting that not everyone can exercise pure unfettered choices – that's just not how life is.

Both these approaches to power are all too often simply a way of passing the buck. I believe they also misunderstand the real community power that most people want. Most people don't want to be able to run their own school. They want to pay their taxes and for someone else to do it, and to do it to a high standard, whilst they get on with their jobs, so that they can pay their mortgages and put food on the table, all the while trying to carve out enough downtime with their families.

But when public service delivery goes wrong they want enough personal or community power to be able to sort it out – or to insist that someone else does.

Ed Miliband's vision of One Nation, the belief that we can achieve more through our common endeavour than we can on our own, holds the key to building stronger and more resilient communities. One Nation Labour will put the great men and women that live at the heart of our communities at the heart of our politics – the people who, week on week, get in touch when things don't work, who put their head above the parapet to argue back, who take the time to visit an elderly neighbour in need of support. One Nation politics means grasping their hope and amplifying their voice. Ed has called for a better politics for Britain, and that is what we are creating: a movement that enables people to bring change to their communities, a movement that is earning back the trust needed to change Britain.

If the head teacher of Small Heath School – just one person – can achieve so much, just imagine what an army of community leaders could do. Hope creates the possibility. Leaders are skilled in creating reality out of possibility. With a little help along the way – my job – community leaders can turn the community's hope into big changes. That's the One Nation job description I'm working to, and, together with the people of Small Heath, I am hoping to make a difference in my community – which I am so fortunate to serve.

Shabana Mahmood is MP for Birmingham Ladywood. She was born in Small Heath, Birmingham and educated locally before reading law at Oxford. Before being elected she was a barrister specialising in professional indemnity litigation.

4. In service to the common good

Dan Jarvis

I've had the great honour in my life to be part of two institutions whose role in this country I hugely respect. The first is the British army, which I joined in 1996. The second is the Labour Party, which was the reason I left fifteen years later – when I became MP for Barnsley Central.

They are, of course, two very different bodies – though I'm sure Labour whips have at times longed for military discipline on the back benches. But they have one great thing in common. Both, at heart, are based on the idea of service.

When I joined the army, I felt it offered me the best way of doing something that I believed in – making a contribution to the country. And the experience of service and of conflict taught me a lot. It taught me about the value of the team, and what could be achieved through collective effort even under extreme pressure. It taught me the importance of selfless commitment, good morale, standards, and the values of decency, compassion, loyalty, integrity and trust. Though challenging, it was inspiring to serve alongside those who were prepared to accept huge personal risk and sacrifice, not for personal gain, but in order to serve a common good. Through it all, that sense of service, along with the camaraderie, sustained me through some very difficult times.

When I took my first steps in politics it seemed natural that I should seek to serve the Labour Party, because I knew this idea of service was also at the heart of our party. We were founded on the idea that government should be the servant of the common good, that power and opportunity should not be restricted to the few, that democracy meant something more than the dominance of a small elite. Our basic impulse was, and is, that the state should be the servant of the people, not the other way round.

But each political generation needs to work out in their own way how to give practical expression to that idea of service. Without losing an ounce of our desire to bring progress to the country, we have to keep on refining and perfecting what it means and how to achieve it – because the problems that our country faces change with each year, and the weapons we can use to tackle them also change.

Ed Miliband's leadership has given us a renewed mission: to rebuild Britain as One Nation. For me, this idea sums up both the continued urgency of Labour's historic task and the philosophical shift we are making in the way we pursue it. It is both a destination and route map on how to get there. One Nation politics requires government, the private sector and civic society to work together to build a Britain in which everyone can and does play their part. It matches our desire for progress with a greater recognition of the place of the individual – not as a counterpoint to society, but as a part of it. It matches a spirit of innovation in the ways we deliver services with a reinforcement of the state's role in guaranteeing equality and progress.

For much of our political past our party concentrated on economic issues and basic social concerns. We gained historic protections for workers. We built a national health service that is an example for the world. We built a social security system that helped millions avoid poverty and destitution. We invested in education so that all young people had the opportunity to learn and to get on, regardless of their background. Together we fought the giants of ignorance, want, squalor, idleness and sickness. Those achievements represented a huge stride forward in the history of this country. We should be immensely proud of that legacy – but we should also measure our own actions and ambitions against it.

These victories, great as they were, were not, of course, the end of history. One Nation politics means both protecting – cherishing – places and institutions such as the NHS which bind us together, and recognising what needs to change. All of us serve in our party today because we know that our country still faces enormous challenges. There are 2.3 million children living in poverty in the UK. Income inequality is among the highest in the industrialised world, as we have seen the living standards of all but the very richest squeezed for year after year. We live in a country where each year thousands of elderly people needlessly die from the cold. We face the prospect of hugely disruptive climate change. And many of these things could be seen as resulting from failures of the market. I think Adam Smith himself would choke at the idea that the amount of money received by some bankers is the natural result of free and fair competition. But more than that, these things are simply wrong. They represent avoidable suffering and avoidable injustice, which we can and must fight to put an end to.

We serve in the Labour Party because we believe that these problems need action, because we do not believe that inequality and unfairness are part of some ordained natural order, and because we know that we will not – and cannot – succeed as a country while the gap between rich and poor is growing wider and wider. Ultimately, we serve because we believe in the power to bring change of politics, the people of our country and our party. The world still demands that we be ambitious. But how do we realise this ambition?

Labour is changing

In the past we concentrated on using the state, both to deliver services and to manage the economy. It was a powerful and in many ways effective tool, but it was also a blunt one. It helped people, but too often it also treated them like the subjects – it was something that did things to and for people, but not with them. And it focused very strongly on the material conditions of life. This is what colleagues like Jon Cruddas have characterised as the 'economistic tradition' in Labour: a world view centred on how much was being spent on different groups.

One Nation Labour is based on a broader idea of service. It recognises that those 'economistic' or materialist concerns still matter, especially as living standards are being squeezed as never before. But it also incorporates an understanding that the well-being of society involves more than material considerations – that, as Ed Miliband said in his first speech as Labour leader, there is more to life than the bottom line. It understands that we need to develop a richer, more nuanced vision of the world we are working towards, one that better encompasses – for example – relationships, community and autonomy, and our own individual definition of our needs and aspirations.

Economists sometimes talk about 'economic man' – a homogenous, 'rational' clone, interested in nothing but maximising his own selfish interests, defined in economic terms – a mythical figure that is rarely seen in real life. I sometimes think Labour thinking has owed too much to this particular individual. One Nation Labour provides the opportunity to lay him to rest.

In practical terms that means a transition in our thinking about the state and its relationship with citizens and communities, finding ways in which it can more closely reflect what people want and need. This would involve, for example, co-production – the development of services in collaboration with the people who use them – becoming the norm rather than a think-tank talking point. (Steve Reed sets out more detail of this approach in his chapter.) It would also mean adopting a more tailored approach to getting people back into work – as seen in the emphasis on effective training and jobsearch support in the compulsory jobs guarantee programme proposed by Ed Balls and Liam Byrne. And it means 'whole person' care, as Andy Burnham and Liz Kendall have advocated – based on what people want and need, not what is convenient for the state.

Such an approach also means – as Stephen Twigg has argued – a 'whole child' education, based on much more than test results, and encompassing key aspects of character development, such as leadership, resilience, self-management and the ability to work in a team. It means a greater emphasis on localism, as Hilary Benn has long advocated. It means a greater concern for some of the more intangible sinews of community – including preserving and improving our public spaces – parks, leisure centres and libraries. It means, in short, working with a richer, more nuanced, vision of progress, built on a more human scale.

The politics of the common good

Community innovation and engagement – a politics of the common good in which everyone takes part – will be at the heart of One Nation Labour policy-making, and central to the way we will seek to govern.

Ed Miliband has talked about the importance of government working together with individuals, families and communities to rebuild Britain as a country where – as in the armed services – we are able to overcome enormous obstacles through our common endeavour. This means practising a politics of the common good, combining an over-arching social concern with a sense that government must play a role as backstop, however light its touch. Co-production will not mean an unfunded outsourcing to the community. For us the state should match respect for local autonomy with a willingness to act where there are unacceptable disparities or 'market failures' – there will be no self-serving insistence that injustice is nothing more than the natural order of things. Our politics is one of democratic practice, where there is a negotiation between different interests looking for common ground. Our form of service is more responsive, because it is based on giving people the power to shape their lives.

One Nation Labour is moving on from the straitjacket of seeing the market as the only innovative alternative to the state. Of course there are times when the private sector can and should play a role in delivering public services. But while the market can be a powerful tool, it remains a tool, not a panacea. Too often it has been used to privatise accountability but not risk. Too often the cost of the supposedly efficient private option has been more than the alternative it replaces. Over and over again, most recently in the NHS, we have seen the market touted as the solution, and shoe-horned into the system, when at the very least there are serious questions about its practical effects. A decision to privatise should be made with the right attitude: rather than being a negative decision – using the market to reduce the role of the state – any move to introduce the market should be made on the positive grounds that we know it will do better.

We will not abandon the market, but we will leave the starry devotion to the Tories, because the test for One Nation Labour is the public interest. We will subject the public sector to the same rigour, but feel relaxed about using it where it works better. We will try to make state services more responsive to communities, more

innovative and more efficient, by involving users –
looking for inspiration and alternatives to civil society
and the cooperative movement.

At a fundamental level, this agenda is about
challenging who has power in our country. There were
many achievements of the last Labour government of
which we should be enormously proud. But we now have
a leader who also recognises that we did not do enough to
change the balance of power in Britain. In Ed Miliband
we have a leader who knows that giving people control
and autonomy is both an objective in itself – an important
element of the society we are working for – and a means
to that end: it can be a powerful tool for ensuring that
public services deliver what is needed as efficiently and
effectively as possible. Our agenda is based on a fearless
willingness to rein in those who have become too
powerful at the expense of fairness and the common
good. It recognises that there cannot be one rule for a few
and another for everyone else. The rules must be made for
all and apply to all.

We should delight in the opportunities this offers us.
With our roots in cooperatives, in trade unions, in the
movement for worker dignity, this agenda belongs at the
core of Labour's identity. An unresponsive, leviathan
state was never part of our founding vision. And
embracing this new spirit is revitalising us as a party and
as a movement. It is helping to bring us closer to the

people and countering the growing disillusionment with politics and government. And it is giving us a measured response to the needs of the many, underpinned by our core values, not a project dreamed up by the few.

A One Nation Labour approach to public services and the way government relates to individuals and communities does not mean replacing one fashionable, restrictive ideology with another. There is a useful discussion to be had, for example, over where and how to draw the line between local control and a post-code lottery. The only rule for me is that the debate should rest on an undiluted commitment to our mission to be in service to the common good, and on openness, innovation and rigour.

In Tory rhetoric, freedom and the market are often little more than useful camouflage to justify greed and the rule of the strong. By understanding the nature of service, embracing the change we need, and delivering a better politics that ensures everyone can play their part, One Nation Labour is making our vision stronger and more democratic. It is why our party exists. It is about a more perfect form of service.

Dan Jarvis is MP for Barnsley Central and the shadow culture minister. He entered Parliament in 2011 having previously served in the British Army for fifteen years.

5. Made by the many: Britain's wealth creators

Catherine McKinnell

At a recent constituency surgery I was visited by a local businessman who shared with me his past five years of anxiety and misery. He and his family firm had entered into a loan arrangement with their bank involving an interest rate hedging product, known as a 'swap'. His family, and the many who rely on them for employment, have been reeling from the consequences ever since. It stirred in me a deep sense of anger and frustration at the injustice of their treatment by their bank and financial advisers, and at the broader impact of this issue on our society and economy. I determined to do whatever I could to put things right.

It was this same determination to make a difference that led me to seek election to parliament back in 2009 as the representative for Newcastle North. This is the area where I was born and where I have family roots on both my mother and father's sides. I still live here today with my young family. My constituent's situation touched a particular nerve because it brought home to me how things have changed since the days when my grandfather's construction firm was building houses in the west end of Newcastle. His business was an integral part of the community during my childhood years.

My grandfather

As a young Irish immigrant, my grandfather travelled to England looking for work, starting out as a builder's labourer. He was sought after for his long arms as he could easily carry a whole toilet! He went on to establish his own building construction company, which built hundreds of quality affordable homes across Newcastle. He was always a fairly private man, and I only realised at his funeral just how loved he had been – the crowds who came to pay their respects spilled out onto the street. But it was when I stood for election that I really understood what he had meant to so many people.

As I went round knocking on doors I encountered a whole variety of people who either knew him, worked with him, or lived in one of the houses he had built. The fondness and respect people had for him was evident in every encounter. I loved hearing the stories of families who had bought one of his houses as their first home together, many of whom still lived in the same house, and talking to people who were proud to say they had worked with him all their working life.

My granddad loved this country and the opportunities
it gave him. He used to say that you shouldn't grumble
about paying taxes, because it means you're making
money. Despite building hundreds of houses in the city,
he lived until the day he died in the very first one he built.
He always drove a small car, wore a brown trilby hat, and
saw a week's holiday a year as more than sufficient, and
he grew nothing but potatoes in his back garden (good
Irish ones, he used to say).

He was honest to his core and had no truck with time
wasters. For him, even talking was a waste of time – he
valued listening more highly. He worked hard and
expected the same from others, but treated those he
employed fairly and with respect. He used to give every
one of his staff a chicken at Christmas, and would
regularly sub his workers – rather than see them get into
trouble with the Wongas of the day.

My grandfather's reputation was paramount to him. If
anyone was unhappy with his firm's work, he would do
everything he could to rectify the problem. If people
remained dissatisfied he would give them their money
back. He was a grafter, and was as willing to unblock a
sink on a bank holiday call-out as plan a new estate of
houses.

Debt was something he took very seriously, to be
avoided at all costs. Sometimes, during the recessions
when business was very bad, he would pay suppliers with

personal funds. He put people before profit, and valued above everything else honesty, integrity and respect for people – whether that was his customers or his employees. M Grady Builders provided quality housing for families across Newcastle for many years – and is proof that moral integrity can go hand in hand with running a successful business that provides employment for many.

Putting his values into practice

So that was the example that I grew up with, and the one that informed my strong sense of social justice. And as a child I also developed an awareness of how fortunate we were compared to others in the world. Like many in my generation I grew up with Band Aid and the harrowing images of children dying in Ethiopia and West Africa, in the twentieth century, because of a lack of food. This inspired my passion for Fairtrade, which is ultimately what brought me into politics – the idea of business not just as a route out of poverty, but as a good in itself, particularly when it has at its core the good of society as a whole.

Fairtrade had a strong UK hub in the North East through Traidcraft, an organisation based on Tyneside that was instrumental in setting up the Fairtrade Foundation and Fairtrade Mark. In the 1980s it began to emerge from its roots in sales at the back of churches on a Sunday, to become a major organisation; and I was gripped by the idea that consumers should be able to choose to buy goods safe in the knowledge that the producers had received a fair price for their supplies, and fair pay and treatment in return for their labour. As the elected Finance Officer in the student union at Edinburgh university I saw through the introduction of Fairtrade tea, coffee, sugar and chocolate in all university retail and catering outlets. This was a huge step forward for the Fairtrade brand.

I represent a constituency which has areas of real affluence but also of genuine deprivation. I am always amazed when I visit schools in the area, as it is often students in the most deprived parts of Newcastle that demonstrate the most acute concern about unfairness and injustice around the world, and are most passionate about doing something about it. I am often left pondering the best ways to harness this collective ambition and turn it into action for real change. I also ask myself what I can do to improve the life chances of the young people in these communities.

One of the first things I did when elected in 2010 was to introduce a Private Member's Bill on apprenticeships and skills. I was determined to do something that could give hope and opportunity to young people in my region, who, I could see, were going to bear the brunt of this

Conservative-led government's slash and burn approach. My Bill proposed a legally binding commitment from companies bidding for public contracts worth over £1 million to provide skills training and apprenticeships in return for securing the contract. It represented a small change that could make a big difference, by providing jobs, training and a future for thousands of aspiring apprentices. I am proud that in his speech to Labour Party Conference last year Ed Miliband confirmed that the next Labour government will ensure that large contracts will be awarded to companies that will train the next generation with apprenticeships: government procurement needs to concern itself with more than the simply buying of goods and services; it must be about the public and private sectors joining forces to build One Nation together.

Rebuilding the economy

Which brings me back to my constituent. His family company has a long and proud history of doing business in the region, but it has been brought to its knees by a financial institution with which it banked for more than four decades. It is a company – like that of my grandfather before it – which provides good, skilled employment, and takes pride in its high quality service and loyal staff, and yet it has been totally let down by our banks.

This is exactly the sort of firm that is central to the One Nation vision of a strong, sustainable economic recovery built to last – one that is made by the many and not just the few. As a country we should be supporting this kind of business. Rebalancing the economy has to mean the banks helping firms like this to grow, generate employment, invest in new machinery and assets, and fulfil their growing order books. It cannot be right that a good local employer with a proven history and huge potential has instead been pushed to the brink of collapse as a consequence of a 'swap' deal that it was urged into by its bank.

Banking reform was central to Ed Miliband's conference speech in 2012. He told the big banks that they needed to start serving businesses in this country rather than expecting businesses to serve them. He put them on notice, calling for an end to the two nation system of the banks and the rest of Britain: we need a One Nation banking system as part of a One Nation economy.

There has never been a more crucial time to rebuild the system so that it works for our small and medium firms. Not only are they the lifeblood of our economy; they are also a locally rooted source of employment and aspiration. I have talked to the banks in my local area, and I have been heartened by the efforts that some of them seem to be making to reach out to new businesses, entrepreneurs and small and medium sized businesses in the region. Yet there is still an evident mismatch between the banking system and the real economy.

The banks need to loosen the stranglehold they still exert over local employers up and down the country – some aspiring to start up, others looking to expand and grow. It is time to acknowledge the mistakes that have been made, and to take the action necessary to put things right. Not only is this vital to restoring trust in the system, it is also necessary if we are going to enable such companies to power economic growth and create much needed employment. It is only through small and medium companies like these that we'll be able to tackle the living standards crisis facing Britain.

A One Nation approach requires solutions that work for the whole economy, wherever a business is based. I want my children to know that the opportunities to succeed are here for them, in the region in which they were born. My granddad travelled a long way to find the opportunity he needed, but if we are to succeed as a nation we must harness the potential of every region. The North East is currently suffering one of the highest unemployment rates in the country. Yet it is a region with a proud history as the engine room of our industrial revolution, and has immense untapped potential.

Earlier this year Ed Miliband set out more details

about the plans that Ed Balls and Chuka Umunna have been developing for a British Investment Bank, which will provide long-term and patient capital for British businesses, especially those just starting up. He also outlined linked proposals for a new network of regional banks, which will have a mission to serve their local region and that region alone. These will be banks that know your region and your business – banks you can come to trust rather than mistrust.

Ed is determined that One Nation Labour will be the party of the small business and entrepreneur as much as the party of the public sector. He recognises that a thriving small-business sector will play a crucial role in our future success as a country, as together we build our economy with tens of thousands of businesses, not just a few.

So we need financial institutions that work for the greater good of the economy and wider society, harnessing the potential for economic growth that exists in every corner of Britain, instead of leaving whole swathes of the country behind. We need a banking system that offers a regionally focused source of investment finance that can be put to work for the good of the real economy – not one that is engaged in predatory behaviour, generating profit out of failure. A 'fair trade' banking system, if you like, the kind my grandfather would have benefited from.

One Nation stands for a financial system that works
for businesses like that of my constituent, who was
successful but was badly let down; an economic system
that works for people like my granddad, who worked
hard, created jobs and opportunity, and gave something
back; a system that enables economic growth and the
generation of employment for our young people. We need
a system that recognises that we succeed only when
everyone plays their part: a One Nation economy that
once more places at its very heart honesty, integrity and
respect for people.

Catherine McKinnell was elected as the MP for
Newcastle North in 2010 and currently serves as a
shadow minister in Labour's treasury team. She lives in
the constituency with her husband and two children, and
before becoming an MP worked as an employment
solicitor in Newcastle.

6. Everyday life and national renewal

Rushanara Ali

The idea of One Nation that Ed Miliband has put at the heart of Labour's mission is important to me because it gives us the means to rekindle a sense of ownership and belonging in our country, a feeling that people have a stake in the future of Britain, and are not being held back.

By contributing to this story of national renewal through our everyday encounters and interactions we can all help to rebuild trust in our politics, and open up better access to political and public power.

If I were asked to give an example of what most closely represents One Nation, it would be the opening ceremony of the 2012 Olympic Games. And I know this also helped inspire Ed Miliband when he was crystallising his vision last year. That ceremony painted a picture of an open, outward-looking and dynamic country. A nation that is proud of its achievements and optimistic about the future. A nation that has travelled on a long journey since its colonial past, when it was resented and mistrusted, and many were uneasy about showing national pride. A modern one-nation Britain.

The Olympics were much more than a passive
representation of twenty-first century Britain. They
actively contributed to a sense of our nation as creative
and participative, a country in which we are all able to
play a positive role. That extraordinary Olympic summer
of sports, culture and music not only showed Britain at its
best; it gave everyone a chance to take part. As Ed
Miliband put it at last year's Labour Party Conference,
the Olympics 'put up a mirror to Britain and showed us
the best of ourselves'. The reason the Games were such a
success was that 'we came together as a country and we
worked together as a country'. They gave us a glimpse of
the country we can be.

As we begin to rebuild our country we need to apply
those lessons and that experience.

For me, the One Nation project has three main
aspects. First there is the essential task of renewing
politics in local communities – giving everyone an
opportunity to take part, as well as a sense that they can.
The second task is the strengthening of public services, so
that they bring us together and ensure that everyone has a
stake, while at the same time harnessing the best ideas
and innovations within and outside of government. And
the third crucial element is the creation of the necessary
conditions for economic recovery – one that is made by
the many – through backing new industries and
technology in our interconnected world.

Renewing politics in local communities

My constituency is a stone's throw from the Olympic Village. It represents modern, diverse Britain at its best – and sometimes worst. As its newly elected MP I am only too aware of the challenges we face in building a new kind of politics that speaks to people's ability to make a difference.

In this context I often think of Max Levitas, a man who is now in his nineties. Max was born in Dublin in 1915, the son of Jewish immigrants who had fled the anti-Semitic pogroms of Tsarist Russia in 1912. In 1927 extreme poverty forced the family to emigrate to the East End, where as a young man of twenty-two Max was to become a veteran of the Battle of Cable Street. Two years before that, when only twenty, he had been fined £10 for his anti-Mosley activities: the British Union of Fascists had called a meeting in Hyde Park, and in protest Max had white-washed Nelson's column, calling on people to go to the park to drown out the fascists. In 1939, when he lived in Brady Mansions in my constituency, he was convenor of a twenty-one week rent strike. He went on from this to become a longstanding Communist councillor in Stepney.

In the 1960s and 1970s Max stood alongside Bengali men like my father to fight the National Front. Today he stands alongside me, as we once again take to the streets, this time to resist the English Defence League's attempts to stoke up racism and anti-Muslim hatred. Still going strong, Max speaks with charismatic vigour of the social ideals that defeated National Socialism and Mosley's fascists. His story is the story of the East End, inspiring so many and reminding us of all the struggles that built the city and nation to which we could belong.

I think also of an elderly lady who survived the Blitz but overnight lost her family, and of the many other stories of sacrifice and loss I have heard.

The East End has long been a place where people have made history and fought for social justice – going back at least to the 1880s, when the match-girl strikers took action against their appalling working conditions at Bryant and May, helping to pave the way for the trade union movement, the suffragettes and the welfare state. East End people have been an inspiration to the great social reformers of the past – who took on and developed ideas born in East London, and drew on them to change this country for the better.

Many social reformers started out in these streets, including Clement Attlee, who worked in the famous Toynbee Hall settlement, and my mentor and political inspiration Michael Young, whom I first met through a chance encounter, when I was still at school and he was revising his 1950s study *Family and Kinship in East London*. Michael was a hugely innovative thinker on political and social policy, and author of Labour's 1945 manifesto, *Let Us Face the Future*. As Tony Blair recognised, he was 'one of the guiding hands of Attlee's great reforming government'.

Michael set up over sixty organisations during his lifetime, including the Open University, the Consumers' Association and the Patients' Association. Through his work I came to learn about the power of ordinary people and communities to develop new ideas that could transform society for the better. I was fortunate enough to be involved in his later work in establishing organisations like Language Line (a national telephone interpreting company designed to support people with language problems), and Futureversity, a charity that promotes arts and education-based independent learning.

Ed Miliband has spoken of the need to build new relationships in every community of Britain. One Nation politics is about more than electoral politics; its aim is to connect our party to people's everyday struggles, hopes and aspirations, to provide a voice for those who feel voiceless – the old man who is fearful of rapid change in his community, the young unemployed graduate who made her family proud but cannot get a job, the recession-struck cab driver who has to wait hours before he can make a few pounds on a fare. We want Labour to once again be a community organisation, one that opens up politics to people from every walk of life, and stops its drift to become a game that is open only to a narrow elite.

Under Ed's leadership we have begun to build the skills and capacities of the next generation of leaders at every level of the community, and to rediscover a way of campaigning that builds a strong sense of belonging, solidarity and common purpose. One example, as Shabana Mahmood describes in this book, are the street champions in her constituency in Birmingham. A political party that is truly in touch with the public is able to draw new energy, ideas and a sense of purpose from such direct experiences.

Campaigns such as London Citizens, Movement for Change and the UpRising Leadership Programme – a cross-party charity of which I was co-founder and Ed Miliband is Patron – are all examples of link-ups between political activism and the capacities of citizens, of drawing on people's skills and talents to work with political parties and bring about social change.

Harnessing the best ideas and innovations within and outside of government

My constituency sits between the glittering towers of the City of London and Canary Wharf. Yet 42 per cent of our children live in poverty – the fourth highest rate of all UK constituencies. And there is a chronic housing shortage, with 22,000 people chasing 2000 social housing properties in the borough each year.

The Olympics delivered a huge opportunity, and a sea change in attitudes towards our country, our sense of national pride and our sporting ability. Yet unemployment actually increased in my constituency during the period of the Games. It is impossible to walk its streets without seeing the energy, dynamism and drive of local people, but this energy is not enough. People need a government that's on their side, nurturing talent and creating opportunities. But right now they see a government that is abandoning them. Britain is now less socially mobile than it has been for decades: nearly one million young people are out of work, while the top 1 per cent of our society hold a greater share of our national income than at any time since the 1930s. Despite the efforts of the last Labour government, life expectancy decreases at every tube stop as you head east on the London Underground.

To deliver social justice and extend opportunity we need a radical overhaul of the ways in which our public services are delivered. A One Nation Labour government will reform our public services so that the people who use them, and the people who work in them, can play a part in shaping them.

Taxpayers must get value for money. It must be an

obsession of the left to ensure that every penny of public money is spent effectively, and that public servants are held to account through greater transparency, accountability and proper stewardship of public money and how it's spent. This is the challenge set by the zero-based spending review announced by Ed Balls.

And this will be greatly helped if, rather than focusing on the delivery of outputs from state to citizen, we grasp some of the ideas that have been pioneered by organisations and individuals rooted in their local communities, including those who work in public service. The insights and experience of front-line workers such as doctors, nurses and teachers are all too often overlooked by top-down initiatives. Government's role should be about identifying the best of these ideas and scaling them up. One such example is Studio Schools – schools that seek to address the growing gap between the skills and knowledge that young people require to succeed and those that the current education system provides. This bold new approach, already piloted, teaches through enterprise projects and real work, and could have a key part to play in developing the talents of the 50 per cent of young people that our current education system leaves behind.

And there are many other innovative organisations, including the UpRising Leadership Programme, which is dedicated to nurturing and developing young people between the ages of 19 and 25, so that they can become the next generation of effective leaders across the public, private and voluntary sector. The programme offers a unique combination of leadership training, mentoring and support, and currently works with 150 young people each year, across East London, Birmingham, Bedford and Manchester. It has an alumni network of over 450 emerging leaders. This, as with many other projects, has the track record and potential to be scaled-up and replicated nationally.

Backing new industries and technology in an interconnected world

Ed Miliband has been clear that rebuilding Britain as One Nation means a recovery to which as many of us as possible contribute, and an economy that works for ordinary people. To deliver this, Ed Balls and Chuka Umunna are setting out how we will support new industries and technology in order to generate long-term growth and earn our place in the global economy. Emerging technology and social innovation hubs are beginning to create a highly skilled, high-tech economy that creates sustainable and well paid jobs, capitalising on the talents of our young people.

Our creative industries enrich the life of the nation and

make a significant economic contribution. Today's East End artists and creative workers continue to support the area's longstanding belief that everyone, regardless of background, should have free access to art and culture. Henry Moore's *Draped Seated Woman* (the Tower Hamlets cast of which has been the subject of recent controversy about plans for its sale) was based on his wartime drawings of people sheltering from the Blitz in the Underground at Liverpool Street. Recent research by Nesta suggests that the wider creative economy could be worth up to 9.7 per cent of UK GVA; and the creative industries account for around £1 in every £10 of the UK's exports. These industries must be supported so they can inspire an inclusive, sustainable economy.

An enlightened industrial strategy is essential to drive green growth and create jobs in a long-term, low-carbon economy. In an era of anaemic growth in the UK, we need to build on our trading relationships with Europe and America, but also look beyond to the Asian, African and South American economies that are on the march, some of which have striking levels of growth. One of our greatest legacies as a party has been to lead the fight against global poverty, and there is no doubt that as emerging economies grow, we have much to be proud of and much to gain as their economic partners of the future.

Conclusion

One Nation Labour gives us a powerful narrative about rebuilding our communities, cities and country in the wake of the worst financial crisis and recession for decades. It is a call to arms for people to find their voice, and to use their talents and capacities to renew our country.

The ultimate test will be whether or not the great offices of state and corporate power remain within the grip of a small elite. This Tory-led government has shown that it is only interested in standing up for a few at the top; it is irretrievably out of touch with the lives and the values of the many.

We will do our bit in fighting to get this awful government out of office. But Ed Miliband is determined that we will do much more than that: he will lead the next Labour government in achievements of solid and lasting significance. We want to ensure that power, money and resources are shared fairly, and that this is backed by meaningful action that ties the places and communities in which people live to our national story.

Only One Nation Labour can harness this collective public energy and imagination. One Nation Labour will enable us to together bounce back from the political and economic shocks that have so shaken our national confidence.

Rushanara Ali is MP for Bethnal Green and Bow, and the shadow minister for international development. Prior to her election she was Associate Director of the Young Foundation. She worked at the Communities Directorate at the Home Office from 2002 to 2005, and at the Foreign and Commonwealth Office from 2000 to 2001.

7. Minding the gap

Lilian Greenwood

Every couple of weeks I get a text from my eighteen-year-old daughter, Patsy, demanding to know my position on some question or issue that has attracted her attention. 'Why haven't you signed the No More Page 3 petition?', she asks. 'You are voting for equal marriage, *aren't you?*'

She is her mother's daughter. Inequality and injustice make my daughter incandescent with rage, just as they did me when I was her age. Her questions provide a regular reminder of the reason I joined the Labour Party in the 1980s. I saw patients waiting months for operations. People I grew up with on the dole. Our schools, hospitals and council housing were crumbling. I wanted to do something about it.

But I was impatient. We'd just lost the 1987 election, and faced five more years of a Tory government that was deepening the very injustice I wanted to challenge. That's why I went to work for a trade union. I wanted a way to tackle inequality right now. And I found it. Whether it was negotiating a career break scheme that improved the lives of thousands of women workers, or winning an individual discrimination case, I felt I was helping forge a more equal society.

When Labour won power we finally had the opportunity to do so much more. The national minimum wage and tax credits improved the living standards of millions of working families. For the first time homophobia was legally challenged in the workplace. There was real investment in our public services to tackle the root causes of poverty, crime, ill health and educational under-achievement. Our measures helped to lift millions out of poverty and ended the everyday legal discrimination that shamed us all.

But despite those thirteen years of achievement, inequality remains a huge challenge for my daughter's generation. And, however unfairly, New Labour famously came to be seen as being intensely relaxed about the growing gap between the richest and poorest. In an age of austerity, when the new inequality is between those at the top and everybody else, this is a reputation we can no longer afford.

That's why I was inspired by Ed Miliband's declaration that 'in One Nation, in my faith, inequality matters. It matters to our country'. It is both necessary and right that, as we build a One Nation Labour Party capable of winning the next election, we are renewing our commitment to a more equitable distribution of power and resources.

Learning from the past

Under Ed Miliband's leadership we are learning from the
successes and mistakes of the past, and tackling
inequality is a case in point. During the thirteen years of
New Labour government, the very real progress that was
made in lifting people out of poverty, particularly
amongst children and pensioners, was largely achieved
through the tax and benefits system: poorer families with
children received extra income through tax credits, and
poorer pensioners benefited from a combination of
universal and targeted benefits. This boosting of the
incomes of poorer households might have been expected
to reduce overall inequality, but it is not what happened.
We were all better off, but the redistributive effects of the
tax and benefit changes were statistically offset by rapid
rises in the incomes of those at the top.

The right would argue that this growing gap between
the richest and poorest was a function of rapid economic
growth, and as such didn't matter. But Richard
Wilkinson and Kate Pickett showed in their 2009 book
The Spirit Level that it did. More equal societies are
characterised by higher educational achievement and
social mobility, lower imprisonment and drug abuse
rates, and better mental health. Ed Miliband is the first
political leader in a generation to give voice to a genuinely
One Nation view of inequality. He knows that it harms us

all. We simply cannot succeed as a country if we are becoming more divided, if prosperity is not fairly shared, and if too many people have no stake, or a chance to play their part.

And, of course, this is not only about efficiency. It is also about morality. Where there are sufficient economic resources to ensure that everyone has a decent quality of life, those resources should be used to alleviate social misery. It simply cannot be right that in one of the richest countries in the world, where tons of food are thrown away every day, children are still going to bed hungry.

The challenges we face

This argument for action is all the more pressing in a time of falling real incomes and growing evidence of poverty. Claims made by some that inequality was lower in 2011-12 than in 2010-11 miss the point, and even if this is correct, it is indicative of little more than stagnation in the economy – which has caused incomes to decrease for nearly everyone (precisely the 'levelling down' of which so many past Labour governments have been accused). However, the statistics we have so far seen do not register the full effects of the actions taken by the rich to minimise the impact of the higher top rate of tax, or recent changes in the benefit system, including the cutting back of tax credits and the capping of benefit increases at 1 per cent. Analysis published by the Institute for Fiscal Studies in June 2013 shows clearly that this government's policies are leading to a steady rise inequality, not only in 2011-12 but right through to 2015-16. Howard Reed of Landman Economics, writing in the summer 2013 edition of the *Fabian Review*, concluded that the growth in inequality under this government may even outstrip that of the Thatcher era.

Other policy changes are likely to deepen these problems. Instead of tackling Britain's low-wage economy, unemployment and the insecurity faced by increasing numbers of workers, the government is set on watering down employee rights; among its proposals have been the introduction of fees for employment tribunals, the ending of legal aid for employment matters, and the shambolic 'shares for rights' scheme.

The case for action to tackle inequality might be expected to strengthen as we see the extension of insecurity to a wider range of workplaces and sectors, while wages remain stagnant or falling. And there has been increased recognition of the ways in which the very wealthy use their power to promote their own self-interest, especially since the spotlight has been shone on tax avoidance by both individuals and corporations – causing particular revulsion as shocking numbers of families come to need the support of food banks. But the argument has not been won.

The political challenges we face are significant, but there are also opportunities. Labour was born from the nineteenth-century struggle against inequality in the pursuit of dignity, and in the twentieth century the Labour Party established itself as the most powerful force in Britain for organising working people for the cause of social justice. One Nation Labour means a renewal of this politics: it draws on our legacy of political organising; it seeks new ways to implement our values of fairness, decency and community action in a much changed political landscape; and it gives everyone a chance to take part.

Standing for these values opens up a very clear dividing line from the Tories, and it offers a hopeful and inspiring choice for voters. One Nation Labour stands for a society where the emphasis is placed on the common good, strong public services, shared prosperity and collective endeavour – policies far removed from the Tories' unconstrained individualism and laissez-faire economics.

That choice is becoming ever clearer as the next election approaches. The Conservatives' short-lived modernisation project is fading into memory. The past three years have seen a return to the divisive politics of the past. Those who depend on the welfare state are demonised as scroungers or shirkers. Our public servants are denigrated, and rights at work are being cut away. Progressive policies are now treated as little more than barnacles to be scraped off the boat, as George Osborne and Lynton Crosby try to convince middle-income voters that their interests and livelihoods are threatened by those who are poorer than them.

Tory strategy today seems comfortable with the return of Disraeli's two nations, 'as ignorant of each other's habits, thoughts, and feelings, as if they were dwellers in different zones, or inhabitants of different planets'. The attitudes of the current generation of Tory Party leadership could not be further from One Nation Conservatism. These are people who came to political maturity during the 1980s, a time when the gulf between the richest and poorest was starkly rising; and they have devoted their careers to leading a party that is in many ways more right-wing than it was in the days of Margaret Thatcher.

The Conservative majority in the Coalition government can at least claim some measure of consistency: they are keeping to Thatcher's dictum 'let our children grow tall and some taller than others if they have it in them to do so'. But this relaxed approach to inequality poses special problems for the Liberal Democrat part of the coalition, whose manifesto for the last election noted that Britain was 'a fragile society marked by inequality'. Today they cling on to two policies that they claim address inequality – the raising of personal allowances, and the introduction of the pupil premium.

But neither of these proposals has made any difference to rising levels of inequality. Changes to the personal allowance have been more than offset by cuts to tax credits and the increase in indirect taxation. For example, figures compiled by the House of Commons Library after the 2013 budget show that, even with the rises in the personal allowance, the cuts to tax credits mean that a one-earner family with two children on £20,000 a year is now £381 a year worse off than in 2010, and will be £600 a year worse off by 2015 – and that is before the rise in VAT is taken into account. And this is at a time when the highest earners have seen their income tax rate reduced. As for the much touted pupil premium, contrary to initial promises it has been funded by cuts to other areas within the schools budget. At a time when support services are being cut back for some of our most vulnerable children, we must not tire of exposing the hollowness of these arguments.

In light of this poor record in government, at the next general election the Liberal Democrats must ask themselves whether or not they really believe in a politics that addresses material inequality.

Minding the gap

In contrast to all this, equality is at the heart of Ed Miliband's vision: he believes in a country where everyone can play their part. What's more, One Nation Labour's approach to equality can achieve equality without the levelling down of which the right accuses us. (Here it may be useful to note there is an excellent refutation of the levelling argument in Ben Jackson's recent book *Equality and the British Left*.)

One Nation Labour recognises the equal value of every person, and aims to enable them to fulfil their full potential – which requires a fairer distribution of economic resources, wealth and power. People won't be able to take full advantage of opportunities for education or work if they are hungry, or live in cold or overcrowded housing and unsafe and insecure neighbourhoods. Creating the conditions that allow everyone – not just a few fortunate individuals – to enjoy real opportunities means supporting investment in long-term growth and securing a more equitable distribution of wealth: through progressive taxation, a robust system of social security that mitigates the negative impact of economic forces beyond an individual's control, and a fair labour market that protects workers from exploitation.

In the past Labour came to rely too exclusively on the central state, as Tristram Hunt argues in his chapter. One of the lessons of our history must be to return to our role of organising people to have more power. We will create a fairer society when people take more control over their lives.

The last Labour government built an effective system of tax credits that reduced poverty. But tax credits have proved vulnerable to cuts under an unsympathetic government, and low-paid families have seen a dramatic reduction in their incomes as a consequence. At the same time those on lower and middle incomes have seen their real wages stagnate as living costs have risen. As well as securing growth, One Nation Labour will reform our economy so that it can address such defects at source rather than seek to ameliorate them – through what some have characterised as 'pre-distribution'; this will mean policies to encourage investment in the creation of high quality jobs, improved access to apprenticeships and training, and the promotion of a living wage.

We also need to continue the devolution of power from Whitehall to communities and local government, but we must at the same time build on the successes of the last Labour government, and retain a role for a strategic central state as a powerful agent for improving social conditions.

One Nation Labour is our opportunity to make the case for a more equal society, and to set out the role of government in making it happen. In One Nation Britain the rewards of economic success would be shared fairly – not only between individuals, but also between regions and different ages, including my daughter's generation.

It would stand in sharp contrast to the policies of the

radical right, which are designed to take us back to the old politics of 'each for their own and the devil take the hindmost'. When One Nation Labour faces the electorate at the next general election, a renewed commitment to fairness and equality will be at the heart of our case.

Lilian Greenwood was previously an organiser for the National Union of Public Employees (later UNISON) before being elected MP for Nottingham South in 2010. She joined Labour's front bench as shadow local transport minister in 2011, and was made shadow rail minister in January 2013.

8. Investing in our children

Kate Green

I watched in despair as child poverty rose inexorably under the Tories in the 1980s and 1990s. The disgraceful statistic which for me exemplified that poverty most powerfully was the rising number of families forced to bring up their children in bed and breakfast accommodation.

These weren't cosy seaside B&Bs, gleaming clean and welcoming, and with a full English every morning. They were dreary, dirty, depressing, over-crowded rooms, crammed full of clothes, toys and family belongings. Children lived in rooms with a gas-ring in the corner, a shared loo at the end of the corridor, and a disturbed drug-using neighbour on the stairs. These were the conditions in which some of the poorest mums and their children were expected to exist under the Tories.

Children should never be expected to grow up in such conditions. How could they possibly develop and thrive? As a feminist, I was even more angry that the government did all it could to make sure that it was usually their mothers – especially single mothers – who took the blame.

My anger intensified when Social Security Minister Peter Lilley composed and sang a song at the 1992 Conservative Party conference about his 'little list': a well-paid, comfortably housed, powerful man, demonising 'young ladies who get pregnant just to jump the housing queue'. He was rapidly followed by his equally privileged Conservative cabinet colleague John Redwood, who visited the deeply deprived St Mellons estate in South Wales to castigate single mothers. It was despicable behaviour, and lone parents were furious. And they have not forgotten or forgiven the Tories to this day.

In 2000 I was appointed chief executive of the National Council for One Parent Families. It was the best time ever to do one of the best jobs ever. As a key part of its strategy to end child poverty, the Labour government (after a shaky start, when it had axed lone-parent benefits) had set about a programme to ensure that lone parents – the parents who'd stayed to care for the children, the parents who'd often never set out to bring up their kids alone, the parents whose children would, despite their best efforts, be most likely to grow up poor – would no longer raise their children in poverty.

Lone parents knew child poverty was the Tories' shameful legacy. When Labour came to power in 1997, the UK had the highest rate of child poverty of any country in the EU. Child poverty had doubled since

1979. One in three children was growing up below the poverty line.

How the Labour government improved children's lives

When, in 1999, Tony Blair set out a visionary goal for the Labour government to eradicate child poverty in a generation, poverty campaigners were delighted, though some doubted it could be done.

But at One Parent Families, and later as chief executive of Child Poverty Action Group, I had a ringside seat from which to observe Labour systematically implementing policies that tackled some of the root causes of poverty. Labour's strategy worked. By 2010, when we left office, more than one million children had been lifted out of poverty – child poverty stood at its lowest in twenty-five years.

The Tories try to say that Labour's child poverty strategy failed. I am outraged at the way they distort facts.

Tories claim that Labour moved children from just below the poverty line to just above it. But that is not true – income rose in every decile of the distribution group under Labour, not just among those hovering around the poverty line.

Tories claim that Labour thought 'poverty was only about money'. But that is also not the case. Labour developed a sophisticated range of policies that tackled all elements of childhood disadvantage, with policies that were both successful in improving the life chances of the poorest children and popular in reaching all families.

We created Sure Start, improved school standards, supported parents to balance work and caring, tackled smoking, drinking and teenage pregnancy. On 48 indicators of child well-being measured by Unicef between 2004 and 2010, 33 had clearly improved, and only two had got worse.

But it is also evident that in a capitalist economy – where it is money that buys autonomy, dignity, power and choice – income is important. What's more, the evidence is clear: children brought up in families without adequate incomes fare worst on a whole range of measures of well-being. So Labour's child poverty strategy was right to place income centre stage. Increases in child benefit and the introduction of child tax credits lifted hundreds of thousands of children out of poverty.

Recognising that work should be the best route out of poverty, Labour also focused on maximising parental employment. We introduced the new deals (including, notably, the new deal for lone parents – lone parent employment rose from 44 per cent in the mid 1990s to 58 per cent by 2010). Other important measures that ensured that parents were better off in work included the national minimum wage, help with childcare costs, and working tax credit.

I am hugely proud of what Labour achieved in government. We prioritised reducing child poverty. We significantly improved children's lives.

Now, I despair at the return of the Tories' divisive rhetoric. And it's not just rhetoric. This Conservative-led government's policies will have bitterly divisive consequences for families with children. While living standards for many families are being squeezed, it is the poorest who are squeezed tightest.

The Institute for Fiscal Studies forecasts that 1.2 million more children will be in poverty by the end of the decade. That will reverse every inch of the progress which the last Labour government fought so hard to make. Absolute child poverty is rising, while progress on relative income poverty has stalled. (And the only reason that this measure of poverty is not worsening is that middle incomes too have been squeezed tight by the flat-lining economy).

Now the sceptics are again out in force, arguing that in times of austerity we can't afford to tackle poverty. Even Ed Miliband has said that tackling child poverty will be tougher in the next parliament.

But what marks Ed out as a genuinely One Nation leader is that he has insisted that we can still make progress.

We do live in different times, and the different pressures we face today call for different approaches. What distinguishes the One Nation approach is that it recognises that this problem cannot be solved by government acting on its own but needs everyone to play their part and pull their weight.

A new approach to working life

One of the things that we have learnt, to our regret, is just how easy it has been for a malignly ideological Tory-led government to unpick the gains we made. Looking back at the legacy of the last Labour governments, we can see that we didn't anticipate the fragility of our hard-fought gains against child poverty. We didn't sufficiently embed the structures and programmes, and we didn't succeed nearly well enough in gaining broad public support for what we achieved.

So when I think about strategies to tackle child poverty now, when I think about our priorities in the most difficult of economic times, I think about solutions that go to the very heart of the One Nation Society we want to build. I think about what's important in my own life, and in the lives of the people around me in my constituency. This is a reality with which the Tory-led government is utterly out of touch.

I know how much it matters to me to have a decent job that means I can support myself. Yet today, two thirds of the children growing up below the poverty line do so in families where at least one member of the household is working. It is simply unacceptable that going out to work is not enough to ensure that you can provide for your family.

In my own constituency I see the humiliation, fear and despair of parents who cannot find work that pays enough to support their children. I see the desperation of the single mum who came to my surgery, unable to make ends meet. She works 16 hours a week in a sandwich shop, starting at 6 am. Her mum looks after her toddler until his nursery opens at 9 am. She'd love to find a better job, or even just to increase her hours, but there's nothing suitable available.

I think of the mum who works as a carer on the national minimum wage. She's paid for the fifteen minutes she spends with each client, but not for the travelling time between. She'd like to spend more time with her clients. She'd love to take her children away for a break. But she knows she can't afford it.

It is wrong and unfair that parents cannot provide for their children because the workplace lets them down. It is wrong and unfair that part-time work (often preferred by mothers with caring responsibilities) is disproportionately poorly paid. It is wrong and unfair that employment rights have been watered down by the government. It is wrong and unfair that the wages of so many people are too low to support a family – and yet last year the High Pay Commission reported that executive pay at the top of the FTSE100 companies has risen by 12 per cent.

That is why one of the priorities for a One Nation Labour government will be to tackle low pay, narrow the pay gap and end workplace discrimination. And this is not simply because of our concern about fairness; it is because we know that we will only succeed as a country with a recovery that is built to last, one that is made by the many and not just a few at the top. That is why we will work towards a new settlement in the workplace for modern workers – rightly described by Ed Miliband as the real wealth creators. We will seek to empower, entitle and equip workers to be adequately rewarded for the job they do; to have more autonomy over the way they do it; and to be able to progress at work.

There's plenty of evidence of the benefits of a stronger worker voice in decision-making at work – for businesses and for employees – so we will strengthen worker engagement in corporate governance, including on remuneration committees.

And there's plenty of evidence that a labour market based on a higher level of skills is a more sustainable way to reduce poverty. So we will engage employers as partners in designing a young person's compulsory jobs guarantee that provides real jobs, along with the effective training and support that is needed to help people find a permanent position.

And we will be bold in identifying who it is that suffers the greatest disadvantage in the labour market – including disabled people, those from ethnic minorities, women, the young, the old – and taking the radical steps needed to address the barriers they face. This means challenging stereotypes at every level in our education system, monitoring pregnancy discrimination, implementing our legislation on mandatory equal pay audits if sufficient voluntary progress isn't made, tackling the zero hours culture which leaves too many people unsure from day to day how much they'll have to pay the bills, doing what we can to extend the living wage, and refusing the Tories' race to the bottom on employee rights.

Improving the quantity, quality, dignity and rewards from work speaks to the concerns of everyone in our society – as indeed it always has. We still remember with shame and anger the exploitation of workers in earlier centuries, in earlier decades. And today, if we are serious about wanting to eradicate child poverty in a new world order, the longstanding imperative to tackle exploitative working conditions assumes an even larger importance. Simply, we cannot tolerate a situation where the product of people's labour is distributed so unfairly that parents cannot meet the cost of raising their kids.

Meanwhile, I dread the coming winter for the poorest families. Children will need new school uniforms and shoes. The heating will need to be switched on. It will be dark and cold, parents will be reluctant to let their children walk to school, so they'll have to meet extra costs for transport. There will be no money to pay the bills. More will go to loan sharks. More will rely on food banks.

I try to imagine how hard I would find it to have to ask for food, or borrow to pay for the basics. Parents on low incomes have no choice – they have to provide for their kids. How can it be right they should have to face ever more challenges and humiliations?

This is why Ed Miliband and One Nation Labour are right to prioritise access to affordable credit, and to promise that we will tackle exploitation by loan sharks. We can also ensure that no child goes hungry, that every child eats a healthy lunch or breakfast at school, and that we help families meet the cost of living. Protecting children must be a priority – and yet the Tories' priority is to give half a billion pounds worth of tax breaks to married couples, which won't even benefit most parents who care for children.

Poor families are all too often accused of wanting luxuries for their children. Sure, they want to buy their children a mobile phone so they know where they are when they're out. They want to buy them birthday presents. They want access to the internet. They want to take their children swimming and for a burger afterwards. But the problem in Britain today isn't that parents want too much for their children. The problem is that we have a government that has a poverty of ambition for most people in this country. In one of the poorest areas of my constituency, just 12 per cent of children are able to swim. Their parents can't afford the classes.

If we are to become One Nation, we cannot tolerate a society in which poor children cannot access what most of us take for granted, where childhoods are curtailed and blighted. That's why One Nation Labour makes ending material deprivation a priority. It is committed to building an economy and society that provides an adequate income to every parent, so that children can make the most of their childhood.

Investing in our children's future

But concerns about child poverty are not solely concerned with the here and now. We must also think about the adults our children will become. If we are to have a decent future as a nation, we must invest in the potential of all of them. We must fulfil what Ed Miliband has called the promise of Britain, where everyone can play their part.

I think of the constituent who is so worried about her oldest son's student debt. Now her youngest son says he won't go to university. He doesn't think he can afford to. His mother wants her son to study and get on, but deep down she agrees with what he says. She's angry, unhappy and utterly ashamed – she feels she has let her son down.

I talk to the members of my local youth parliament. They are anxious about the cost of public transport. Their older brothers and sisters benefited from the Educational Maintenance Allowance introduced by the last Labour government to help support those in post-16 education, which made a big difference to their families. Now that the Tories have abolished EMA there's nothing to help with their fares. They can't travel to neighbouring schools for shared after-school clubs because they can't afford the journey.

I think about the part played by a great education in the opportunities I've had. I was lucky to go to a good comprehensive, with excellent teaching and lots of free extracurricular activities. I didn't have to leave university thousands of pounds in debt. Every child has the right to develop to his or her full potential. And we all benefit if they do. That's why Labour must ensure that no child misses out on education because their parents can't afford for them to participate. That's why the government's trebling of tuition fees was so unfair.

We can't be one nation, a nation in which everyone participates to the full, if we fail to ensure that every child has the chance to play their part. Children must be given opportunities to thrive, to enjoy their childhood, and fulfil their full potential. Nor can we be a nation in which everyone has a stake if we have a government more interested in playing political games to divide our country than in bringing us together to solve our problems. Investing in our children is economically sensible and morally right.

This Conservative-led government does not believe it can or should to anything to end child poverty. But One Nation Labour will work together with people of Britain to find new ways of making progress towards this historic mission.

Kate Green is MP for Stretford and Urmston, and shadow spokesperson for equalities.

9. Power to the people

Steve Reed

Within weeks of my election as Leader of Lambeth Council in 2006, the whole community was shaken by a spate of teenage killings. Gangs, mostly of teenage boys from poorer backgrounds on council estates in and around Brixton, were involved in drug dealing and attacking each other with guns and knives. Young people in part joined the gangs for protection against attack, but they then quickly became involved in escalating levels of violence and crime, which destroyed their lives and the communities around them. Mercifully, this was a very unusual situation. But the inability of traditional services to tackle this problem taught me a stark lesson about what is wrong with public services and why they need to change.

While youth, housing, criminal justice and police services had failed to make a big enough difference, parents in the community were not prepared to stand by while their children's lives were ruined. The mother of one teenage gang member, a black woman involved in a local church, led a group of youths to a police consultation meeting and demanded funding for the

community-run projects that were far more successful at
stopping gang crime than public services had been. Over
three years her group, working with barely any resources,
got sixty young people out of gangs – far more than the
council had managed. And yet, when she had asked the
housing managers on her council estate how she could do
more to help, she was told to leave it to the professionals
because they knew best. That sums up where some public
services go wrong: those running them assume they know
everything – and that those using them know nothing.

That is wrong, and under Ed Miliband's leadership
Labour is beginning to understand that top-down public
services fail to either understand the needs or harness
the insights and resources of the communities for whom
they exist.

Services fail to adapt because citizens – the people who
use public services – lack the power to make them change;
so they become stuck in doing what they've always done,
even when it's no longer effective. We have become
wedded to fixed ideas of what particular services do.

Instead, One Nation Labour is developing an
approach that sees public services as social and economic
investment to enable citizens and their communities to
realise their potential, and improve their quality of life
and life chances. That means reform to correct a longstanding imbalance of power and narrowness of vision.

Driving this approach is the key insight of Ed

Miliband's conference speech last year: One Nation is a country where everyone plays their part. That is not just an objective, but also a means by which to make it happen. People should have more power and control over their lives, so that everyone feels able to play their part in building strong communities.

The action we eventually took in Lambeth to curb escalating youth gang crime was to share the council's power with the communities that were most affected. They'd already shown how much they could achieve without funding; combining the council's staff, financial and other resources with the community's insights in finding solutions that worked was a logical development. The Young Lambeth Cooperative is a new youth services trust owned by the community that is taking control of the council's multi-million-pound youth services budget. The trust will work with affected communities to help them define the support they need then bring it in. Instead of parents feeling terrified and frustrated with public services that are slow to respond, they will have the power to influence decision-making by working in a new partnership of equals. The process needs to go further, to encompass other factors that lead some young people into joining violent gangs, but the approach of sharing power with citizens can improve services right across the board. There are examples of this working in different services up and down the country.

Changing the old model of public services

Public services today operate in ways that are very similar
to when the welfare state was set up after the Second
World War. Professionals identify problems in people's
lives and then attempt to deal with them, through services
that are fairly rigidly structured to deliver specific
support or interventions. Yet British society has been
transformed since the period immediately after the war.
We are far less deferential, far more diverse ethnically and
culturally, people have the kinds of choice over the goods
and services they consume, and the lifestyle they choose,
that would have been unimaginable decades ago. People's
aspirations and expectations are very different.
Communities and their needs are fluid and ever-
changing, but we remain straitjacketed in a top-down
approach to public services that no longer fits the kind of
society we've become.

It is not just in youth services that empowering citizens
can be transformational. Older people want home-care
services that are flexible enough to suit different lifestyles
and cultural backgrounds. I have met with residents
demanding change in the way parking controls operated.
On a housing estate residents were angry with the slow
repairs services and the filthy state of communal areas
like landings and staircases. I saw problems like these
raised in meetings where the people with the power to

make change happen – councillors or managers – were often the ones who understood the problem the least, because they didn't live with them. Change was slow to come if it came at all, and it depended on finding someone both willing to listen and determined or powerful enough to wrestle change out of organisations that preferred to let things go on as they always had done – because that way was easier for them.

For people worried about a badly run bin collection service this can be frustrating. For people who depend on public services for things that affect their life more profoundly it can be debilitating if those services go wrong. If you live in social housing, rely on home-care services or are unable to find work, then major aspects of your life are controlled by the people who run the services on which you depend.

Over time – or, even worse, over generations – forcing people to rely on decisions made by others takes away their self-reliance and their ability to aspire to a better life – they can no longer see a way to break out of their situation. Dependency is not created by over-generous benefits, as the Tories claim; benefits are not generous at all, and most people forced to live on them for an extended period of time are on the breadline. The culture of dependency is the result of forcing people from poorer or more excluded backgrounds to live by the decisions of people who have not shared their life experiences, and who have never asked them what they really want. To break the cycle of dependency and give people back the self-reliance and aspiration we've taken away, we have to give them back control over the decisions that affect them.

There's another problem, too: public services are often designed to deal with problems in people's lives, rather than to prevent those problems from happening in the first place. A preventative model of public services – both because it costs less and because it improves people's quality of life – is one of the core principles set out by Jon Cruddas in his June 2013 speech to the Local Government Association. Such a model, would, for example, involve helping people to tackle behaviours that lead to ill health or crime; or helping people to develop new skills that will keep them in work; or providing more, and earlier, help to parents who are struggling to bring up their children safely. Prevention is better than cure, and it is cheaper too.

Citizens need control over the outcomes that public services are trying to deliver. Whatever resources are available, people need the freedom to define for themselves what they want to achieve; and public services should then help them to achieve what they have chosen, rather than continuing with things that people would not choose for themselves. That will lead to working with communities in new ways and in new areas, such as in developing community energy generation as an alternative to high energy bills, as Brixton Solar Energy has done, or supporting credit unions as an alternative to loan sharks, or – as we're doing in Croydon – developing employment strategies that harness the networks of people that exist around individuals in order to help them find jobs. Citizens need the power to change what public services do, how they are delivered, how different services join up, and who delivers them.

Sharing power

How we go about sharing power varies from service to service. Council housing tenants can elect boards that appoint housing managers, so that they are directly accountable to tenants. They can even, as has happened in Rochdale, become shareholders in a tenant-led housing co-operative in which frontline staff also have a place on the board. Turning Point, a major social enterprise providing support for people with mental ill health, trains service-users to engage with others in the same position, so that their views can influence the way services are delivered. Labour-run Oldham Council helps unemployed people get back to work by asking them what support they need rather than forcing them onto standardised – and usually unsuccessful – training courses as prescribed by the Department for Work and Pensions. Lambeth council has mutualised its disability resource centre, which is now providing a much wider range of support, in new ways, and has strengthened job security for employees. Edinburgh Council is creating a city-wide childcare co-operative to increase availability and lower costs. There's no one way of empowering citizens, the approach has to be tailored to the people, the place and the outcome you're trying to achieve. But there is a litmus test: if citizens have more real control over their lives as a result, progress has been made.

Sharing power has a radical and transformative effect on people and communities. By involving groups of citizens in the decisions that affect them we strengthen the relationship between people within their community as well as between people and the services they use. Instead of banding together in frustration to oppose things they don't like, people come together to define and achieve shared objectives. Instead of atomising communities, we strengthen their ability to tackle the problems they face, making them more resilient by building social capital. By allowing different communities to try new ways of tackling problems, we create more space for innovation that can be shared to improve lives more widely. For politicians this not only means letting go, it means taking a different view of risk: trying to control everything too tightly and imposing uniformity stifles creativity and breeds inefficiency, as we fail to maximise the value of the public resources being deployed.

This more co-operative model of public services demands radical change from government at both the local and national levels. Over time, organisations become protective of their own existence and their own power. Most councils are structured into giant directorates such as Housing or Children's Services, with tiers of directors, assistant directors and senior managers. It is difficult for elected councillors, let alone frontline staff or people using their services, to challenge these powerful interests. If we really want to empower citizens we need to break down these powerful silos and return to flatter, less hierarchical structures. Once that has been done, councils and communities can find new ways to reshape services and make them directly accountable to the people who use them. Frontline staff, too, find it liberating to be freed from the multiple layers of management and bureaucracy that prevent them from doing things differently.

We also need to break down the barriers that exist across different parts of the public sector operating in the same locality, including councils, the NHS, DWP, education, and the criminal justice system. If we want to join up services in ways that make more sense to people, we need to first get organisational barriers out of the way.

This requires a new relationship between national and local government. We need to identify all the public resources spent in a particular locality, and then negotiate single-pot deals that focus on agreed outcomes. A Labour government would wish to see outcomes such as reducing inequality, increasing employment and the supply of affordable housing, but we would leaving the methods for achieving these up to the locality and its council. Pooled budgets, with a much wider scope than Total Place or community budget pilots, make it easier for communities to join up services differently, and focus resources on delivering the outcomes they want; while direct accountability gives citizens the power they need to drive change faster.

Local government must become an enabler that brings together communities and the service providers and resources from right across the public sector that can help them achieve the outcomes they want. Whoever provides the service, local government must remain the guarantor of high standards of quality, financial probity, safety, and access for everyone with a right to use a particular service. It also needs to retain the right to intervene if service standards slip below an acceptable level, and would need to offer back-office services like finance, HR and IT to community-led services, to prevent duplication of cost. Because resources are always limited while demand is not, councils need to retain political responsibility for allocating budgets. This does not exclude models of participative budgeting that involve local people, but ultimately there has to be a means of arbitrating between competing demands, and elected councillors are best placed to do that.

One Nation Local

From all this comes a new kind of politics, and an enhanced role for elected councillors. Instead of an alienating politics that requires people to abdicate responsibility to politicians who then take all the decisions for them, we can create a more bottom-up, open and pluralistic politics that involves people in the decisions that affect them. Instead of feeling a recurring sense of betrayal, a sense that politicians fail to deliver on the promises they make, citizens can assume more responsibility for making the change they want to see. Because directly accountable services can only work if information and data is fully open, citizens will need more access to the information that guides decision-making, and more opportunity to challenge and interrogate it, and use it to innovate. Advances in new technology, including social networks and customised online access to services and information, offer limitless opportunities for approaches like this to flourish.

None of this means people that will have to run their own services; it simply means that the professionals who run them will be more accountable to the people who use them. Nor is it about replacing professionals with volunteers. Volunteering is a welcome bolt-on to public services, but it cannot be the core of how public services are run. The skilled and talented people who work in our public services also often feel frustrated that existing structures don't allow their experience to drive change. The point of sharing power is to recognise that both the professionals and the people who rely on their expertise have something of value to offer.

People will give their time to influence decisions if they believe those decisions have a direct and significant impact on them or their loved ones. Vulnerable people who rely most heavily on public services will often need help to participate in decision-making that affects them, but there is always a way to do that – such as involving relatives, carers or advocacy groups. The aim is to enable everybody to play their part.

As decision-making and power become more widely distributed there arises a new opportunity for political parties to engage with the communities they seek to represent. The work of Arnie Graf in developing community organising in the party, and Movement for Change, shows how this might happen. In this book Shabana Mahmood, Rushanara Ali and Gloria De Piero offer their own examples. Local parties will be able to be involved at every point where people are taking decisions that affect their lives – on housing boards, community trusts, school governing bodies, and in campaigning for change. Instead of confining themselves inside town halls, all councillors would need to be out and visible across the whole community – as the best of them already are. They would have a new role in identifying unmet needs and linking them up with the resources that can meet them; and in being involved in decision-making at the community level, as well as scrutinising and sharing best practice across a much wider and more diverse pattern of service provision.

There is no magic wand that can make austerity disappear overnight. Ed has made clear that the starting point of the next Labour government is that we won't be able to reverse the cuts in day to day spending unless it is fully funded from savings elsewhere or extra revenue. We will have fewer resources to work with, but – as Jon Cruddas has also argued – by reforming what the state is and how it relates to people we can offer dramatic improvements in people's quality of life; we can breathe new life into the traditional Labour values of fairness, co-operation and opportunity.

We need a co-operative approach to create a new partnership with citizens and communities to develop an alternative to decline in our towns, cities and rural areas by making them more socially and economically productive. Putting people – and especially the most marginalised – back in control of their lives unlocks self-reliance and uncaps aspiration, allowing people to build a better future for themselves. This is not just a theoretical argument. Many Labour councils, including those in the Cooperative Councils Network – set up by me in 2011 and launched by Ed Miliband – already offer a test-bed of new ideas the next Labour government can learn from. One of these lessons must be the need to trust local government and communities to get on with the job without endless interference from Whitehall.

Usually central government imposes cuts on local government. But Ed Miliband recognises that no one has better experience of how to do more with less than Labour council leaders. So he has asked Sir Richard Leese, Leader of Manchester Council, to head a new Task Force which will advise the next Labour government on how to reform and develop public services in an era when there is less money around.

One of the big dividing lines emerging in politics today is between those who believe power should be concentrated in the hands of a few at the centre, and those who believe power should be distributed throughout society so that decisions better reflect people's experience and meet real needs. Centralisers versus localisers is not an argument about 'big state' versus 'small state'; it is one about how the state, whatever its size, relates to and is accountable to citizens.

One Nation politics means sharing power more equally so that everyone can play their part. It involves strengthening relationships between people within communities, redirecting scarce resources to where they can make a bigger difference, improving people's experience as employees, and tackling economic decline by making our communities more productive. While the Tories want to roll back the state, One Nation Labour will change the role of the state, so that it is controlled by and serves the people who rely on it.

One Nation politics is about bridging divides and bringing people together so that they can achieve more and participate more fully in society. We recognise that co-operation, not just competition, is a driving force for positive change. We will work together with the people of this country and their communities to rebuild and revitalise politics so that we can transform lives for the better. To do that, Labour must trust people enough to do what no party has done before – to win power so that we can give it away.

Steve Reed is MP for Croydon North. Previously he was leader of Lambeth Council, where he pioneered the co-operative council approach to transforming public services. He is patron of the Co-operative Councils Innovation Network, and in 2013 was appointed OBE for services to local government.

10. Our common life

Rachel Reeves

The Kirkstall Festival takes place every summer in my
Leeds West constituency, and this year's theme was
'How Green is Our Valley' – echoing the classic
novel and film *How Green Was My Valley*, which
longingly recalls the lost life of a Welsh mining
community. But the turn to the present tense, and a
collective voice, is deliberate and determined. For me, this
reaffirmation and renewal of community through pride
in a place, both its past and its potential, is what One
Nation Labour is all about. This spirit of people working
together for a common purpose – invoked so effectively
by Ed Miliband in his speech to the party conference last
year – is at the heart of Labour politics today.

Kirkstall's rich history and resilient optimism, just
one of the countless intertwining threads that make up
our continuing national story, reminds us of the great
resources of energy and commitment our country can
draw upon.

Organised annually by the Kirkstall Valley
Community Association, and run entirely by volunteers,
the festival is the largest community festival in Leeds.

Local families, churches and mosques, as well as pupils and parents from nearby schools, all come together to contribute to a fabulous day of fun that draws large crowds from the surrounding area. Entertainment this year ranged from stand-up comedy and cabaret to the Leeds Morris Men and new South Asian Dance. And I'm pleased to say the local Labour Party branches played their full part as well – minding stalls, running tombolas and helping as stewards.

It's a brilliant feat to pull off at a time when everyone feels that their free time and family finances are under such pressure, and public sources of support are so scarce. The average wage last year in Leeds West was £19,240 and, as elsewhere, has been falling in real terms – and 30 per cent of children in Kirkstall are living in poverty. And as if this isn't enough, the City Council has had to make cuts of £55 million this year, on top of £145 million in 2010-11 and 2011-12. But Kirkstall has weathered tough times before, and it's worth exploring that history a little to see if we can find lessons for these times.

Working together

Kirkstall Abbey, in whose grounds the festival is held, was first founded in the valley of the River Aire in 1152 by the Cistercian Order, who were set apart by their emphasis on self-sufficiency and manual labour. As one early Cistercian explained, 'We put great effort into farming which God created and instituted. We all work in common, we, our lay-brothers and our hired hands, each according to his own capability, and we all make our living in common by our labour'. Cistercian monasteries served as centres of work, education and welfare for surrounding communities, as well as pioneering new methods in agriculture, metallurgy and hydraulic engineering.

The Abbey was closed in 1539 (J.M.W. Turner is one of many to have painted its famous ruins). Some historians have argued that the dissolution of the monasteries may have stamped out a nascent industrial revolution in England. But the corn mill constructed by the monks continued to turn, and by the late sixteenth century the mill race was being used to power iron production and the manufacture of agricultural tools. Meanwhile, in the wake of the Reformation, non-conformism flourished in the area. Wesley himself is said to have preached in the small chapel at the iron forge, and across Leeds the Methodist message of self-reliance and social responsibility proved a powerful galvanising force among growing numbers of the working poor.

In 1779 the forge was taken over by two farmers, George Beecroft and John Butler, at the instigation of

Betty Beecroft, George's wife and John's sister. According to local historians, it was this 'determined and enterprising' woman who took personal charge of the forge for the first year of its new operation, and with new investment it was turned to the manufacture of iron axles for horse carts. Thus began an extraordinary period of industrial innovation and expansion, as more and more workers were employed at the forge in the manufacture of axles for railway trains from the 1830s; car, lorry and bus axles from the 1920s; then tank axles and other contributions to the war effort from the 1940s (when women became a major part of the forge's workforce, and the works had to be camouflaged to confuse aerial bombers).

At its peak the forge provided around 1800 direct jobs, and supported many more. Leeds City Council built a new 'sunshine estate' next to nearby Hawksworth Woods to help house the increasing numbers of families moving into the area, with new schools, shops and a park. After the war, a growing South Asian community settled in Kirkstall and neighbouring Armley, enriching the area's cultural mix.

But times got tougher with the waning of the post-war boom. Crucial connecting rail stations at Armley, Kirkstall, Newlay and Apperley Bridge fell victim to the cuts proposed in the 1965 Beeching Report. During the 1980s and 1990s the forge, like so many manufacturing employers in Yorkshire and around the country, struggled to secure the investment needed to survive in increasingly competitive global markets. In the 1990s it was taken over by an American multinational which ultimately closed it, relocating production to India. Some claimed this signalled the end of what had been the longest continually used industrial site in Britain.

Fortunately, Leeds City Council had the foresight and imagination to preserve the abbey as the centrepiece of a municipal park that it created in the midst of what could have been seen as an area of industrial decay; this is now used not only for the annual festival but as a venue for monthly deli markets, open-air Shakespeare and, last year, a brilliant homecoming concert by the Kaiser Chiefs. As a result Kirkstall remains a popular residential area for many working in Leeds city centre, as well as students living in shared housing.

But on the Hawksworth Woods estate unemployment rose, shops closed, schools suffered, and drug use by young people became a problem. Under the last Labour government, investment in local services and support for low-income families provided a lifeline for many in the area – with housing brought up to decent standards and Police Community Support Officers helping local people get crime under control. But that lifeline has become frayed as the community suffers another cruel reversal – from the Tory-led government's cuts and economic negligence.

What history teaches us

Yet the ongoing popularity and success of the Kirkstall festival demonstrates that a sense of belonging and responsibility to contribute runs deep in this country. Our passion and potential for good people to come together and achieve extraordinary things – something that drives Ed Miliband's vision of One Nation – can be seen just as clearly in local events like the Kirkstall Festival as in great national events such as last year's Olympics. By building and strengthening our local communities we build and strengthen our country. When people take responsibility – and have the chance to play their part – it acts as a reminder to us in the labour movement of what we are fighting for, and how best to fight for it.

The festival itself is the product of local voluntary initiative. But it cannot be taken for granted that these kinds of events will continue to thrive, particularly at a time when the economy is stagnating and becoming more polarised, and when government is abdicating its responsibility and looking out for only a few people at the top. We have to worry that the kind of spirit that sustains the Kirkstall festival will be sapped as people have less time and energy to put into their family or community, and the spaces for public life are closed or commercialised; such a spirit is difficult to sustain as people's lives drift further apart, and their sense of responsibility to one another is weakened under the pressure of increasing insecurity and widening inequality.

We need to work together to safeguard that spirit – in Kirkstall and in every community in Britain. For this we need a One Nation Labour government that believes in everyone playing their part. We need an active state that will secure the preconditions for a strong society and flourishing communities. We need its support for struggling families, the freedom to innovate in local services, and for the protection of shared facilities and spaces such as libraries, parks and nurseries. And we need improved employment opportunities and fair rules for our economy – rules that help underpin our responsibilities: for those who can, to seek and accept work; and, for businesses, to pay their taxes and treat their customers and employees decently.

One Nation is not something that can be imposed by the state from the top down. It has to be made by the many not the few. But it does need a government that is ready to play its part – and sometimes take a lead.

The Kirkstall festival is a wonderful example of the energy and activity of ordinary people coming together to improve their own lives; it is the kind of community activity we need to engage with, learn from and harness. Indeed, the labour movement was born out of the long history of collective self-help that included trade unions and friendly and cooperative societies – a history that also includes the Salvation Army, whose values my grandparents taught me about, and whose band played Jerusalem and Amazing Grace at a festival service in the abbey. This history taught people the necessity of harnessing the power of democratic government, locally and nationally, to support and enable the work of building a better society – but history also teaches us that the state can never substitute for, and should never supplant, the active role that individuals, families, communities and voluntary associations will continue to play. For me, One Nation Labour is about re-learning and re-applying that lesson in the twenty-first century.

Another powerful illustration of the potential we can tap into is provided by the living wage campaigns we have seen gathering pace around the country in the past few years. The living wage campaign is about so much more than money – it is also about the dignity of work and the value of family life. And, as Ed Miliband has reminded us, this idea didn't come from politicians, it came from working people.

I'll never forget the pride with which Fran Massey, a cleaner at Manchester College, told me that, having successfully fought for a living wage for herself and her co-workers, she could now buy her children the shoes they needed to compete in basketball championships, and afford to go and watch them play.

The living wage is also, of course, a powerful symbol of, and a real foundation for, the fairer economy we need to build – working families will be less reliant on state spending to lift them out of poverty if they are earning a fair wage that they can live on.

One Nation Labour recognises the need to reshape our economy from its foundations. And this includes government doing what it can to promote and spread the living wage – as Labour councils around the country are already doing through their procurement powers and local influence. A future Labour government will take on this task at the national level, through measures such as requiring greater transparency from big employers, and using the fiscal benefits of better pay to support investment in training and productivity.

But it is also critical not to lose sight of what is so valuable in the actual process of employees, trade unions, businesses and communities organising, campaigning, and bargaining for a living wage themselves – a process that can open the door to so much more than the very real improvements it can achieve, through involving and empowering individuals and forging powerful new solidarities. Ed Miliband has established this as a principle of a One Nation economy: we will only be able to build prosperity when everyone plays their part.

A strong society

We need to seek out and nurture in the Labour Party
itself this spirit of active participation, and dynamic and
deepening relationships with wider society, which can
power and sustain bottom-up change. Of course it is
already something that has long been the lifeblood of
the Labour Party at its best – as brilliantly exemplified
by my predecessor as MP for Leeds West, John Battle, a
principled Christian socialist and dedicated community
organiser, and a man from whom I have learned so
much. And today we are learning again that, even in
opposition, we can be part of the change we wish to see
in the world – especially from the work that Iain
McNicol and Arnie Graf have been doing to spread
good practice and ideas around local parties through
embedded community campaigners. This approach to
politics strengthens our determination to get to work
right away on changing the country, instead of waiting
for a general election and the chance to return to
government – important though that is. And the more
work we put into One Nation politics while we are in
opposition, the better chance we'll have of winning
that election - and the better government we'll be when
we do.

The unfinished story of Kirkstall shows that power
to change the world also lies outside Westminster and

Whitehall, and that in opposition or in office we must learn how to tap into people's energy and zeal for community and belonging. For the inspiring spirit of activism and fellowship that we saw at this year's Festival isn't something that is only in evidence for one day each year. Through the decades, the people of Kirkstall have sustained a sense of pride and purpose in the face of adversity and lazy assumptions of inevitable decline.

Over the years, residents of the Hawksworth Wood estate have used whatever funding they could get to create their own safety nets, from a YMCA that helped young people with severe problems, to Hawksworth Older People's support ('HOPS'), which provides a bus service to shops, lunch clubs and bridge tournaments. There is also a formidable Community Association, out in force at the festival – with whom I was last year able to successfully campaign to re-open the local post office. And earlier this year we had the good news that Hawksworth Wood would receive a £1 million 'Big Local' grant from the Local Trust, on the basis of a community plan for improving the area as a place to live.

When the Forge closed, local residents, businesses, and civil society organisations immediately set to work with the landowners to develop a plan to regenerate the brownfield site that was left. As MP for the area John

Battle championed this plan, along with local Labour councillors, and when I took his place in Parliament in 2010 I was determined to see it through. Our hopes suffered a setback when George Osborne's deep cuts to infrastructure investment put plans for financing the restored rail link into doubt. But this year Leeds' Labour council approved an alternative funding package that should allow works to start next year. The plan promises to bring over 2000 new jobs to the area, with modern new office spaces, cafés and shops, and over a thousand new homes. A new railway station will restore the sustainable transport link lost after Beeching. The river bank is to be cleaned up, and the historic mill race and listed workers' cottages will be restored.

We are opening a new chapter in the story of Kirkstall. The life lived in common, and the shared work of sustaining it, goes on. Drawing on the sources of hope and renewal that lie in its past, and the hard work and community life that that continues in Kirkstall today, local people can look forward with new confidence to a better future. The same can be true of Leeds, Yorkshire and our country as a whole – if we in the labour movement continue to fulfil our unique role of bringing out the best in Britain.

Rachel Reeves is MP for Leeds West and shadow chief secretary to the treasury. Prior to being an MP she was an economist at the Bank of England, the British embassy in Washington and at a retail bank.

11. One Nation Labour

Tristram Hunt

Last year, Ed Miliband's conference speech galvanised the party and began reshaping the political consensus. With that single, striking phrase, 'One Nation', he was able to offer a critique of the existing social order under the Tories, whilst simultaneously offering the hope of a better one under Labour. Its great achievement was to be both radical and conservative: it provided an alternative political economy that spoke to contemporary concerns over the economic crisis, living standards and the nature of change, without retreating into nostalgia.

Yet to grasp the full nature of Ed's argument we need to situate that speech within the context of three important prior interventions. These form the basis of the political architecture that defines our One Nation programme and provides the contours for a new approach to policy development.

First, there is the concept of the 'Squeezed Middle', which articulates the problem that will define the next election: how to arrest the decline in living standards for low and middle earners. This cost of living crisis has become more acute under David Cameron, but median wages for this group were flat as early as 2003, a trend that continued throughout the recession and beyond: even as the economy flirts with a return to growth there appears to be no sign that real wages are set to improve.

Second, there is Ed Miliband's persistent and determined call for a more 'Responsible Capitalism'. This provides our aspiration and our destination; and a vision of the fairer, more equal society we wish to build.

Finally, there is the idea of 'predistribution', which outlines the Labour Party's new political methodology – our process of moving from Squeezed Middle to Responsible Capitalism.

However, as any historian will tell you, 'One Nation' is far from a new phrase. Stolen – as Ed was the first to acknowledge – from Benjamin Disraeli, arguably the Conservative Party's most celebrated champion of the aspirant class, this is an idea with a clear and defined political lineage. To fully appreciate the ways in which it speaks to the condition of Britain today (and indeed, to the condition of the Labour Party), it is helpful to start with a look at the historical antecedents and ideological currents that helped to shape Ed Miliband's 'One Nation' politics.

Catching the Tories bathing

Disraeli first articulated his 'One Nation' philosophy not, as is sometimes thought, during his infamous, brandy-

soaked marathon speech at Manchester Free Trade Hall
in 1872. Rather, it was when, as an out of favour young
politician and jobbing author, he published his 1845
manifesto-cum-novel *Sybil or the Two Nations*. By then
Disraeli was the de facto leader of the fledging Tory
'Young England' movement, which argued for a return to
the social conservatism and paternalistic duty of pre-
industrial England. *Sybil*, then, was deliberately intended
as a distillation of his and their political philosophy.

In the novel Disraeli lambasts the greed and division of
the great nineteenth century industrial cities –
Manchester, Birmingham and the first industrial city of
them all, Stoke-on-Trent. There could now exist within
one city, he protested, two entirely different nations,
'between whom there is no intercourse and no sympathy;
who are ignorant of each other's habits, thoughts and
feelings, as if they were dwellers in different zones, or
inhabitants of different planets'.

These two nations were 'formed by different breeding',
fed by different food, and governed by different laws.
They were 'the Rich and the Poor'.

Of course Disraeli's indictment was far from a lone
voice of criticism. From Gaskell to Dickens, Ruskin to
Marx, the poverty, division and rampant inequality of the
industrialising cities featured in the work of many mid-
nineteenth-century writers. So, as we approach what
often can feel like Victorian levels of inequity today, it is

quite natural that we look to this era for political inspiration.

But the question remains why One Nation? Why, given the intellectual riches on offer, should Ed Miliband choose, as Disraeli himself might have put it, to catch the *Tories* bathing and walk away with *their* clothes?

The reason is that, on so many levels, it is Disraeli's analysis that best chimes with our own – not least in his response to Queen Victoria's 1851 gracious address, when he famously said 'This too I know. That England does not love coalitions.'

Indeed, a proper understanding of Disraeli shows that in certain extreme epochs it is possible to be both conservative *and* radical. We are currently enduring one such era.

Challenging the consensus

Despite signs that we may be finally clambering out of recession, we remain in the eye of a volatile and unpredictable economic storm, brought about by excessive faith in the economic orthodoxies of neoliberalism. And what makes Disraeli so interesting is that he, like Ed Miliband, was motivated by a healthy disrespect for the political and economic orthodoxy of the day.

In both *Sybil* and his earlier novel *Coningsby*, the

target of his ire was the laissez-faire, night-watchman state propagated by the 'Manchester School' of liberal conservatives. Rather than the barren exchange of the cash-nexus, Disraeli stressed the ties that bind; he believed in a moral conception of society beyond the narrow confines of the marketplace.

This attitude is typified by Stephen Morley, the radical agitator in *Sybil*, who roundly condemns the 'great cities' where 'men are brought together by the desire of gain'. Such men 'are not in a state of co-operation, but of isolation, as to making of fortunes; and for all the rest they are careless of neighbours'.

This division into 'two nations', and the ruinous condition of the urban poor of industrial England, was the social cost of this exclusive focus on economic gain. But, as Disraeli saw, such excessive desire was symptomatic of an *entire model* of capitalism that was failing.

Clearly, Ed Miliband has no interest in replacing the neoliberal consensus with the 'Young England' attempt to restore the lost order of pre-reformation England. However, he does share this one crucial insight with Disraeli. And what is more, this is one of the fundamental lessons we must learn from our recent experience of government: that there is only so much you can do to improve the conditions of working people without also changing the underlying structure of the economic model itself.

Beyond the bottom line

The aesthete and socialist John Ruskin, one of Disraeli's most brilliant contemporaries, offers a further insight from the Victorian era that remains relevant to today's political context – and it is one that Disraeli would have shared: not everything of value is reducible to price, or measurable in pounds and pence.

As Ruskin wrote in his 1860 essay 'Unto this Last':

It is impossible to conclude, of any given mass of acquired wealth, merely by the fact of its existence whether it signifies good or evil to the nation in the midst of which it exists. Its real value depends on the moral sign attached to it, just as strictly as that of a mathematical quantity depend on the algebraic sign attached to it. Any given accumulation of commercial wealth may be indicative, on the one hand, of faithful industries, progressive energies, and productive ingenuities: or, on the other it may be indicative of mortal luxury, merciless tyranny, ruinous chicanery.

This was a critique with which Disraeli – with his distaste for the Manchester School – would have undoubtedly concurred. But even now it has lost none of its force. Because today, the pace of change wrought by globalisation has created a sense of loss and of dislocation amongst many of our communities.

However, the last Labour government sometimes failed to respond to this anguish in anything other than the most urgent economic terms; sometimes we appeared to belittle the concerns of those who were fearful of the pace of change, or who longed for stability and order. As Jon Cruddas has suggested, the government sometimes offered fuel for the caricature that it was collapsing the entire Labour project into an exercise in fiscal transfers.

And as a result of this focus, perhaps it also contracted what R.H. Tawney, writing in his 1931 masterpiece *Equality*, called 'the *lues Anglicana*, the hereditary disease of the English nation' – a 'reverence for riches' that disregarded the socialist ethic of fellowship.

We must learn from all this, from Tawney, Ruskin and Disraeli, and avoid the pitfalls of 'monetary transfer social justice', which doesn't do enough to challenge existing structures and concentrations of power. The materialist Coalition, of course, is utterly incapable of learning such lessons, as it eagerly sets about privatising every public good for which they can find a buyer.

A recovery made by the many

There is a further important way in which the 'One Nation' idea is both conservative and radical. When Ed

Miliband gave his speech in Manchester he also offered a clear and renewed commitment to the party's historic crusade of lifting the life chances of working people. On this he was absolutely unequivocal: inequality matters. Too great a distance between the two nations harms social cohesion and undermines our sense of solidarity, ultimately impoverishing us all. That is all the more the case in an age of gross inequality between the very richest and everybody else.

Anthony Crosland's influential 1956 work *The Future of Socialism* grounded the concerns of democratic socialism primarily in equality – as opposed to public ownership – and since then it has been common to label the dominant strand of Labour political economy as 'Croslandite'. The Croslandite model asserted that the best way of advancing social justice was through accepting a relatively untrammelled version of free market capitalism, and to then fight injustice by redistributing the proceeds of its 'perpetual growth'.

But this model is surely inadequate to addressing our problems in 2015. In particular it lacks a critical stance on the way in which the market concentrates existing distributions of power and inequality. And it prevented us from distinguishing between different *types* of capitalism and growth, leaving us unable to make the kind of economic value judgements demanded by our One Nation politics.

It is particularly important that we are explicit about growth. A return to the kind of growth that is disconnected from rising living standards will no longer suffice.

Any lingering pretence of commitment to the kind of growth we need to see was finally abandoned by George Osborne in the 2013 budget. After failing repeatedly to deliver on promises to revive business investment, he discarded his export-led 'march of the makers' rhetoric and made the centrepiece of his budget a 'Help to Buy' scheme that the Office for Budget Responsibility say will push up house prices, while doing little to increase the house building we so urgently need. There are growing signs that the much delayed recovery is mainly benefiting those at the top, while most families are seeing real wages and incomes continue to fall.

We need growth that reduces inequality, delivers more secure work, is more environmentally sustainable, and above all benefits the regions outside of London and the South East. And this approach not driven solely by a concern for social fairness: Ed Miliband's One Nation economy will enable us to succeed as a country, and create a recovery which is made by the many and – this time – built to last.

An economy that works for working people

Widening the discussion about of what kind of growth we need points to further ways in which our old political economy is lacking: it is unable to offer answers to the basic questions that Ed Miliband has placed at the heart of Labour Party policy in these tough times: how can we make a difference in a restricted economic climate, how can we *change* society?

These questions perhaps make the last idea in the One Nation trilogy – predistribution – the most important one for us to grasp.

Any political party that fails to answer this question is not fit to form a government. Indeed, such is the scale of the economic challenge we face in the next ten to twenty years, that I do not think it is an exaggeration to describe the need to answer this question as an existential challenge – for all political parties.

In this context, a closer look at the tax and benefit system begins to reveal some of the the fundamental flaws in our old political economy. Although our current society is scarred by inequality, this is certainly not because of insufficient concern on this issue in the New Labour years. Far from it. Indeed, as OECD statistics show, New Labour's legacy is a tax and benefit system that redistributes almost as much as the famously egalitarian social democracies of Scandinavia.

In fact, the reason that the UK still has the seventh
highest levels of income equality of the 34 OECD countries
is that it begins from the fourth most unequal starting
point. Its levels of redistribution cannot overcome its
predistribution – the way the market distributes its rewards
in the first place. Put bluntly, we redistribute more but the
underlying structure of our economy is more unequal and
unfair.

A further problem with strategies that rely too heavily
on redistribution is that they often fail to recognise that
resources are useless if people don't have the power to use
them. To put the argument at its simplest, there is no
point in increasing people's entitlements if they feel
marginalised by a society that they no longer recognise or
feel part of, or if they lack the capability to access basic
services. The Labour mission should also focus on
strengthening these communities and demonstrating that
society works best when people work together and share
in each other's fate.

Of course Labour can be proud of our redistributive
legacy, and the fact that our tax credits helped to take a
million children out of poverty. And redistribution will
obviously remain part of the Labour way of delivering
fairness. But we need look beyond that to predistribution.

Our opponents have poured scorn on this idea. But
Britain needs new ideas. And one of the great assets of Ed
Miliband's leadership has been his ability to develop new

ways of thinking, new ways of approaching the many challenges we face. We need to find ways of ensuring that economic power and the proceeds of growth are more evenly spread throughout the economy *before* redistribution – to reform the underlying structure of the economy rather than limiting ourselves to ameliorating its inherent inequality.

This is a significant challenge to the traditional political methodology of social democracy. A predistributive approach gives primacy to reform. Out go flashy new ways of spending money and in come smart, inexpensive interventions that have the power to reshape the existing rules of the market.

The challenge of rebalancing the economy and spreading wealth more evenly in these tough times is an extremely difficult one. But it will be made that much easier if we can offer an authentic story of national renewal, one that is desperately needed at a time of fragmenting identities, political apathy and the increasing drift to a two-nation Britain

But the Labour Party's own renewal is already underway in the policy priorities that Ed Miliband has set out, and the shadow cabinet is working together to develop. And the predistribution agenda is beginning to open up pathways to a One Nation Britain.

In the past year we have set out plans for our gold-standard Technical Baccalaureate, which provides a rigorous vocational pathway for the 'forgotten 50%' who do not wish to pursue the academic route; and for the British Investment Bank, alongside a network of regional banks based on the German model, that will provide finance to SMEs in capital starved regions of the country; and for an amplified campaign to encourage large employers to sign up to the Living Wage.

Perhaps the best example of our plans in this area, however, is our approach to social security and housing. We must be prepared to shift the focus of social security spending from benefits to bricks and mortar – to building houses, not lining the pockets of rentier landlords.

Other proposals to help us find new ways of holding unchecked corporate power to account include putting employees on remuneration committees, and the compulsory publishing of executive pay and corporate tax arrangements, as well as the number of employees that are paid less than the living wage.

In addition, Ed Balls and Chuka Umunna have commissioned Sir George Cox to produce a report on overcoming the corrosive short-termism in British business, and the tendency to suck away investment at crucial points in the growth cycle. And as part of Stephen Twigg and Chuka Umunna's initiative for a One Nation Skills Taskforce, Chris Husbands has highlighted how we might build a more highly skilled workforce, in order to compete in a globalised world on our own terms – as opposed to participating in the ludicrous Conservative pursuit of a low-wage, low skill race to the bottom.

The forward march of labour restarted

We have begun the forward march to One Nation Britain – a country in which prosperity is more fairly shared, and we all work together, backed by preserved and renewed institutions. Although this is a hard task, there are grounds for qualified optimism. That is because many of the answers to the challenges of our current political context – globalisation, fiscally responsible change, the rejuvenation of our political culture – can be found within the uniquely *Labour* contribution to social democracy.

The answer lies in the movement itself: for in becoming too reliant on the state as the only means of mitigating market outcomes, we have neglected our associationalist heritage as a movement of democratic grassroots activists: our history of co-operatives, mutual societies and trade unions. It is by rediscovering this heritage that we can begin to put 'the future in our bones', as Eric Hobsbawm once memorably put it (after C.P. Snow).

So, whilst we are deeply indebted to Benjamin Disraeli for the lucidity of his analysis, and can find a common cause with his dream of a Britain united, the energy to realise our One Nation vision, and transform our communities from the bottom-up, is all our own.

Tristram Hunt is MP for Stoke-on-Trent Central and a shadow education minister.